U0139835

（修订版）

床头灯英语·**3000**词读物

GREAT EXPECTATIONS
远大前程

[英] 查尔斯·狄更斯 / 著

北京理工大学出版社

BEIJING INSTITUTE OF TECHNOLOGY PRESS

图书在版编目（CIP）数据

远大前程 : 英文 / （英）查尔斯·狄更斯著 . —北京 : 北京理工大学出版社 , 2019.9（2021.8 重印）

ISBN 978 – 7 – 5682 – 7408 – 1

Ⅰ. ①远… Ⅱ. ①查… Ⅲ. ①英语 – 语言读物②长篇小说 – 英国 – 近代 Ⅳ. ① H319.4 : I

中国版本图书馆 CIP 数据核字（2019）第 175295 号

出版发行 / 北京理工大学出版社有限责任公司

社　　址 / 北京市海淀区中关村南大街 5 号

邮　　编 / 100081

电　　话 /（010）68914775（总编室）

　　　　　（010）82562903（教材售后服务热线）

　　　　　（010）68944723（其他图书服务热线）

网　　址 / http://www.bitpress.com.cn

经　　销 / 全国各地新华书店

印　　刷 / 三河市良远印务有限公司

开　　本 / 880 毫米 × 1230 毫米　1/32

印　　张 / 5.5　　　　　　　　　　　　　责任编辑 / 李慧智

字　　数 / 88 千字　　　　　　　　　　　文案编辑 / 李慧智

版　　次 / 2019 年 9 月第 1 版　2021 年 8 月第 2 次印刷　责任校对 / 周瑞红

定　　价 / 23.80 元　　　　　　　　　　责任印制 / 施胜娟

《床头灯英语丛书》
编委会

丛 书 主 编： 王若平

本 册 改 编： Oliva Williams

高级编审人员：

1

三千词读遍天下书

　　喜欢读有趣的故事、小说是人类的天性，世界各国的人在对文学作品进行愉快的阅读中不知不觉地掌握了自己的语言，英语学习也不例外。但很多英语学习者都有过啃不动原著的痛苦经历，没读完一行就遇到好几个生词，一页纸上密密麻麻地标注了音标和释义，坚持不了几页只得作罢。

　　反观汉语，我们采取了完全相反的学习模式。在 87 000 个汉字中，3 000 多个常用汉字就能覆盖现代汉语的 99%。在长达九年的义务教育中，这三四千个汉字在我们所读的大量文学作品中成千上万次再现，在超量语境的刺激下，我们对这些常用词的准确含义、搭配、用法烂熟于心，而不会为还有八万多个汉字不认识而烦恼，这使得我们的汉语得以运用自如。

　　同样，在英语的 100 万个词汇中，常用的 3 000 词能覆盖国外日常会话、报刊典型文章、常规工作交流所用英语的 85%，剩余 15% 并不会构成大的障碍，所以英语进阶的关键就是在大量作品的阅读中彻底掌握这3 000 词。

　　本套丛书精选了西方最受欢迎的数十部文学经典，从英国女王，到比尔·盖茨、乔布斯、扎克伯格等都读过其中的作品；丛书由当代美国作家执笔，用 3 000 词以原汁原味的现代英语写成，使你躺在床上不用翻词典就可以津津有味地读下去。走进一部英文小说，你就生活在一个"英语世界"里，读几十本英文名著，相当于在美国生活两年，自然能够获得惊人的语言能力。

推 荐 序

王润霞，《床头灯英语丛书》策划者之一，资深英语教育践行者。1998 年以来她按照自己对英语教育的理解，引导女儿取得了一系列惊人的成绩：2004 年北京市高考理科第二名，托福（TOEFL）673 分（满分677 分），清华大学电子工程系专业和综合成绩排名双项第一，获得 10 多所美国顶尖大学（普林斯顿、耶鲁、麻省理工、加州理工、斯坦福、康奈尔等）的全额奖学金，博士毕业后拿到了麦肯锡、波士顿、贝恩三大咨询公司的工作 offer。

我女儿为什么能在中国的语言环境中学好英语

我女儿是在中国语言环境中学好英语的一个代表，她的经历或许会给国内正在学或准备学英语的人一些启示，帮助他们少走弯路，最终享受到学好英语所带来的益处。当然，你可能会觉得我孩子的情况很特殊，属于个例。但是，我的英语教学体会是：**每个学生都是语言的天才，只要学习方法正确，英语没有学不好的。**这些年我一共带了几百名学生，很多考上了世界名校，如美国麻省理工学院、宾夕法尼亚大学、耶鲁大学、康奈尔大学，英国伦敦大学学院等。**这些学生都是普通的学生，关键是他们背后都站着一个大事不糊涂、肯为孩子付出、和孩子在正确道路上坚持到底的家长。**

当年我沉痛的教训，后来让孩子少走弯路

1978 年我考入哈尔滨工业大学物理师资班，从此进入教育领域，后来阴差阳错地和英语结下了不解之缘。我们那时高考是不考英语的，进入大学之前我的英语水平可以这样描述：词汇量不超过 2 位数，单词读

音都用汉字标注，能把 children 读成"秋得润"，英语课本把"工农兵"翻译成"workers, peasants, and soldiers"。上大学之后，我朦朦胧胧地感到英语比较重要，就开始认真学英语。同时把这个当时非常前卫的信息传递给了我的两个弟弟（其中一个弟弟为本书主编），并给他们买了学英语的书，先后让他们跟着广播、录音机学英语。当时中国经历了特殊历史时期，刚刚恢复高考，我们那年入学的学生年龄和背景差别都很大，有 6 个孩子的父亲，也有 3 个孩子的母亲，我们班年龄最大的 34 岁，我 17 岁。在那个年代，大家都非常珍惜这来之不易的学习机会，但学习语言年龄小还是很占优势的，我的英语轻松地取得了好成绩。转眼两年英语课结束，我们就认为英语学好了，大功告成了。

英语老师在结课时告诫大家要多读英语原版书，我就把原版书买回来，也做了计划，每天都看。第一天，看了一页，发现不认识的词比认识的词还要多，第二天也好不了多少，更要命的是看到第 10 页时已经不知道前面讲的是什么了，生词还是生词……这样坚持了 20 多天，只得放弃。其他大多数同学据说连一周都没坚持到。**多年之后我发现大部分中国人英语学不好的关键原因是所读书的难度远远超出自己的水平，台阶太陡，根本上不去，夭折了。**

转眼到了 1985 年，我大弟弟高考，英语考了 99 分（满分 100 分）。进入大学后由于他英语，尤其在语音方面，很出色，便成为学校英语广播电台的播音员。1989 年他大学毕业，以他主修的管理专业在北京找了一个多月工作都没找到。就在他绝望之际，他师兄建议他用英语这项技能尝试找工作，我说："死马当活马医，去试试吧。"一周之内，他凭借出色的英语能力拿到了许多非常满意的工作 offer，最后选择了一家银行总行的国际部。很快，他的收入和生活条件就远远超过了和他读同一所大学、读的专业比他更辛苦、比他早毕业 7 年的我。当时我女儿 3 岁，我就下定决心将来一定让她学好英语。

有些事，不能"民主"

我小时候最喜欢去乡下大姑家玩儿，大姑父、姑姑脾气都特别好，家里非常民主，孩子们自然都很自由快乐。她们家有5个孩子，我二表姐是她家老三，上有哥姐，下有弟妹。她活泼、聪明、能干，地里的庄稼活、屋里的针线活都做得好。她是村里的孩子头儿，村里同龄的孩子大都不上学，所以她也向父母要求不上学。我姑父、姑姑对她说："你自己可要想好了，现在不上学，将来别后悔。"她回答得斩钉截铁："不后悔，后悔也不怪你们。"处在学龄前的我听了特别高兴，如果她不上学，我就可以随时找她去玩了。岁月飞逝，我上大学后又见过她一次，她当时境遇非常糟糕。因为不识字，眼睁睁看着好机会来了，却没有选择的权利。我怕她怨恨父母，就又重提她当年说过的话："不后悔，后悔也不怪你们。"她哽咽着说："我当时那么小，懂什么，现在后悔又有什么用呢！"她那种哀怨的表情让我难受了很久……

我女儿这代人本来就比较任性，在外面自由、快乐教育风气的影响下，她可不像我两个弟弟那么听话。她英语一直到初一都不好，更不喜欢学英语，有的时候还美其名曰："我是中国人，干吗要学英语呀？"当她向我提出不学英语时，我脑海中就浮现出表姐那绝望的表情。最后我坚守了自己的原则底线：别的事可以"民主"，学英语这件事不能商量，你必须学！

专家的教诲

我在北京大学英语研究会主办、北京航空航天大学承办的《大学英语》月刊编辑部工作期间，负责每期的《英语人物访谈》专栏。在采访这些专家时，充分暴露了我这个理工女的特点，凡事刨根问底，那些专家让我受益很多……我一直铭记着原教育部大学英语指导委员会主任、复旦大学董亚芬教授就儿童英语教育说的一句话："**如果条件不具备（没**

有合格的老师、合适的教材），就不要学，学错了比不学还可怕。"所以我一直没有让女儿去上不合格的英语培训课程，最后实在找不到合格的培训机构，就按照我对英语教育的理解，自己聘请老师办了个英语培训学校，教正确的发音、地道的英语。到女儿高考前，她大概读了类似于《床头灯英语丛书》的英语读物800多本，才有了后来的成绩。也正是有了成功的教育案例，我弟弟（王若平）和我才组织、策划了这套《床头灯英语丛书》。我们聘请了几十位美国作家对世界名著进行改编，邀请国内著名大学的教授审读，力求让中国学习者系统、有效地进行英语输入。

之所以推荐《床头灯英语丛书》，是因为它具备以下特点：

1. 语言现代、地道：由美国作家执笔，以原汁原味的现代英语写成，符合现在读者的阅读需求，使尘封的经典得以复活。

2. 通俗易懂：本套书依据科学的分级体系，用现代英语中最常用的英语单词写成，个别难词配上了简明的注解，让你躺在床上不用翻词典，就能轻松读下去。

3. 选材上乘，情节曲折：当今社会，时间成本是最昂贵的，每个想有所作为的人对于书籍的选择，尤其是外语书，必须谨慎，最好读经典。这套丛书的选材非常注意作品对读者的吸引力，比如：

《吸血鬼》(*Dracula*)：这个故事真吓人，我读完以后好几天没睡好觉。后来我的一个学生说他对英语从来不感兴趣，我就把这本小说推荐给他。后来他对我说："这是我一口气读完的第一本英语书，就是太吓人了。老师，能不能再给我来一本？"

《呼啸山庄》(*Wuthering Heights*)：讲述的是一个骇人听闻的复仇故事，很难想象竟出自一个生活在与世隔绝环境中的女孩之手。

《飘》(*Gone with the Wind*)：很多美国女孩都读过这本书。在美国麻省理工学院，两个读博的女生在谈论如何找到合适的另一半的话题时，师姐是这样向师妹传授经验的："你去仔细把《飘》好好读读，然后你可能就有答案了。"

4. 这套读物构建了国内比较完备的英语阅读阶梯体系：包括儿童阅读、1 000 词、1 500 词、2 000 词、3 000 词、5 000 词、6 500 词等阶梯系列，每个阶梯都有很多本，读者可以根据自己的水平选择一个起点，循序渐进地展开阅读。学英语要有足够大的输入量才能形成语感。我们当年就不明白要大量阅读比较简单的读物后再上台阶的道理，结果白白错过了年轻而又充满学习热情的关键时期，导致一辈子都没办法自由地使用英语。后来在陪女儿学英语的过程中才发现：中国人学英语失败的主要原因是地道英语的输入量远远不足。而语言能力上的获得是一个长期的过程，需要大量的"输入"。没有几百万个甚至是上千万个英文单词的输入，很难掌握英语。人们总指望把某本或者某几本书读完了英语学习就能一劳永逸，殊不知，"微量阅读"是学习英语的致命方式。

5. 配有高质量的录音：这套书所配的录音是标准的美式发音，特聘教育部录音专家录制音频，音质清晰、优美，语速缓慢，非常适合英语学习者反复精听和模仿。在缺乏正确英语语音的中国语言环境下，简单、标准、地道的语音输入量严重不足，是英语学习者发音、听力、口语不好的主要原因。本套书的录音对中国英语学习者而言无疑是雪中送炭。

6. 这套书也得到了国外读者的肯定，我在美国纽约书店注意到美国读者也喜欢这套书，它是在美国少见的中国出版的图书之一。

当被问及英语学习的问题时，我经常会想起当年那些英语专家的教诲。我一直对他们心存感激，是他们的理念让我培养出一个比较优秀的女儿和一批比较出色的孩子，我也愿意把我的体会分享给那些在通向英语自由境界的路上迷茫的人。

王润霞于北京

世界著名翻译家，北京大学许渊冲
教授（左）

教育部第一任大学英语指导委员会
主任，清华大学陆慈教授（左）

教育部第二任大学英语指导委员会
主任，复旦大学董亚芬教授（国内
大学英语教材鼻祖）（左）

在 MIT 参加女儿博士毕业典礼与女
儿合影

原大学英语四六级考试委员会主任，
上海交大杨惠忠教授（右）

名家巨擘论阅读

光学几句干巴巴的英文不行……不要总是把阅读的目的放在提高英文上，阅读首先是吸收知识，在吸收知识的过程中自然而然就吸收了语言。

——许国璋（中国英语教学的鼻祖
历任北京外国语大学英语系主任、外语研究所所长）

用英文思维是许多英语学习者都希望达到的一种境界，因为这是用英语流畅地表达思想的基础。对于一个生活在非英语环境中的中国学生来说，要做到部分或全部用英文来思考的确有很大难度，但也不是可望而不可即。从自己学习英语的经历中，我体会到坚持大量阅读是实现这一目标最有效的途径之一。

——何其莘（北京外国语大学副校长、博士生导师）

对于初、中级英语学习者我特别推荐英语简易读物，读的材料要浅易，故事性要强，读的速度尽可能快一些，读得越多越好。这是学英语屡试不爽的好方法。

——胡文仲（北京外国语大学教授）

要学好英语，就要对语言本身及语言所传达的各种文化信息感兴趣。当你读到或听到别人用简洁的英语表达深奥的思想时，兴奋不已，立即记住，这就表明你已对语言产生了兴趣。没有这种兴趣，难以在语言学习中登堂入室。

简易读物对打好基础极有用，要多读。一是数量要多，至少读40

本。二是要重复读，选出 10 ~ 15 本，读 3 遍。

——梅仁毅（北京外国语大学副校长、博士生导师、美国研究中心主任）

美国脱口秀大王奥普拉·温弗瑞是最富有、最有影响力的美国女人之一，她把读书称作"my personal path to freedom"（我的自由之路），她那句"The most successful people all tend to have one thing in common: They read"激荡了美国年轻的一代。

微软创始人比尔·盖茨说："人和人的生命曲线很不同，突破人生局限的最好办法是读书。"他年轻的时候读了许多科幻小说，现在保持每年读 50 本书的习惯，《了不起的盖茨比》他和妻子读了无数遍。

特斯拉总裁马斯克是个对知识充满渴望的读者。小时候在南非经常受欺负，是科幻小说赋予他灵感和动力，使他创造出新的硅谷传奇。当被问到如何学习建造火箭时，他回答说："I read books."

沃伦·巴菲特在被问到成功的经验时，他指着一摞书说："每天读 500 页，那就是知识起作用的方式，它像复利一样地积累。你们所有人都做得到，但我保证你们中没有多少人会去做。"

脸书创始人扎克伯格 17 岁前很喜欢读科幻小说，现在每两周读一本书，是读书使他保持了永久的创造力，他最喜欢这句："All children are artists. The problem is how to remain an artist once you grow up."

推 荐 语

1. 这套《床头灯英语丛书》，囊括了诸多英语名著，都是我们这代人在青少年时期曾汲取营养、启迪审美、塑造三观的世界文学经典之作，或思想蕴涵深厚，或行文清新细腻，或情节曲折感人，都有很高的文学审美价值和语言学习价值。

要让青少年真正地爱读名著，社会、老师和家长要形成一种合力，从高处着眼，从细处入手，激发阅读兴趣，引导阅读方式，营造阅读氛围，做好高质量的阅读陪伴。《床头灯英语丛书》是阅读经典与实用学习的得兼之作，值得青少年朋友们阅读学习。

——师传宝

中国外语教育研究中心中小学英语教育研究中心秘书长、

英语周报社副总编辑

2. 想学好英语，多读经典好书是捷径之一。《床头灯英语丛书》有语言、有思维、有文化、有审美、有情感、有人生百味。英语名谚说："Reading is to the mind what exercise is to the body." 运动强健躯体，阅读滋养灵魂。快来把阅读变成你的生存方式吧！它将给你一双隐形的翅膀，让你的人生从此自由而丰满。

——陈力

人民教育出版社编审、《义务教育课程标准实验教科书英语（新版）》责编

3. 阅读给我们打开了一扇窗。透过窗我们看到了别人，也看到了世界，通过这扇窗，我们也更好地看到了自己。

——陈新忠

北京教育科学研究院基础教研中心英语教研员、

教育部《高中课程标准》修订组核心成员

4. 我有一位同事，他是数学教师，但英语学得很棒。我曾经问他："你的英语学得如此地道纯正，有什么秘诀吗？"他坦诚回答："我只是读了几本床头灯英语小说。"可见，对于学习英语而言，名著阅读可以起到事半功倍的作用，也完全符合英语课程标准的理念。

——何书利

北京教育学院朝阳分院教师专业发展中心主任、
北京市英语学科骨干教师

5. 20世纪60年代，我也是中学生，曾经阅读过所推荐书目中的大部分简写本，夯实了基础，开阔了思维，增加了兴趣，让我受益良多。我号召中学生朋友们翻开书，一本本读，会大有裨益！

——范存智

北大附中资深英语教师、人民教育出版社新课标教材培训教师、
北京教育考试院高考和会考试卷评价课题组成员、英语沙龙杂志顾问、
北京教育出版社教育科学研究院副院长

导　读

狄更斯，19世纪的文学巨匠，英国文学史上的传奇和骄傲。他的创作以非凡的艺术概括力展开英国社会的广阔画卷，反映了当时人们生活的真实面貌。其作品充满了光辉四射、妙趣横生的幽默和细致入微的心理分析。《远大前程》这部小说情节扣人心弦又感人至深，希望由萌生而至幻灭的过程引起一代又一代读者的共鸣。

善良的匹浦是个孤儿，一天他在教堂墓地遇到一个逃犯，他从家中偷出食物和工具，帮助了逃犯。不久，富有的郝薇香小姐想为其恶毒的爱情游戏寻觅一个男孩，匹浦被选中住在她家，之后爱上了她的养女——骄傲的艾丝黛拉。一天，郝薇香的律师突然前来，告知有个神秘人要把全部财产留给匹浦，匹浦得以到伦敦接受教育，过起了奢靡堕落的生活。在一个风雨交加的夜晚，一位不速之客造访，原来他就是当年匹浦在墓地救济过的逃犯——马格维奇。为报一饭之恩，他把攒起来的钱寄到伦敦培养匹浦。为看一眼自己造就的绅士，他冒险回归，却不幸被捕，死在狱中，财产全部被没收。艾丝黛拉也嫁给了别人。匹浦大病一场，恢复后心灵获得了一种新生。他离开了英国，多年后回国与艾丝黛拉重逢，两人沐浴着朦胧的月色，携手走出已成废墟的郝薇香老宅。

Contents

Chapter 1 Pip and the Stranger ················· (1)

Chapter 2 After a Prisoner ····················· (11)

Chapter 3 A Good Chance for Pip ··············· (20)

Chapter 4 A Present from a Stranger············· (37)

Chapter 5 Mrs. Joe Is Attacked ················· (52)

Chapter 6 Great Expectations ··················· (63)

Chapter 7 Arriving in London ··················· (73)

Chapter 8 A Visit to Mr. Wemmick and Mr. Jaggers········· (81)

Chapter 9 Joe Comes to Visit ··················· (89)

Chapter 10 Pip and Herbert Discuss Love··············· (96)

Chapter 11 Pip Goes to a Funeral ················· (99)

Chapter 12 Pip and the Truth ····················· (106)

Chapter 13 Magwitch's Future and Past··············· (114)

Chapter 14 Pip Visits Estella and Miss Havisham Again··· (122)

Chapter 15 A Safe Place for Magwitch ··············· (128)

Chapter 16 Miss Havisham Realizes Pip's Suffering ····· (134)

Chapter 17 Pip Is Close to Death ················· (139)

Chapter 18 Magwitch's Story Ends··············· (144)

Chapter 19 A Wedding ······················· (153)

Chapter 1
Pip and the Stranger

My real name is Philip, but when I was younger I was only able to say Pip, so Pip became my name and this was what everybody called me. I came from a small village in Essex. I lived there with my elder sister. She was older than me by more than twenty years. Her husband's name was Joe Gargery, who was the village ironworker. My sister raised me because my parents had died when I was a baby. I was not able to remember them at all. Still, I would often go to visit the churchyard, which was about a mile① from the village. They were buried there in the graveyard, and I would go to look at their names on the stones.

One December afternoon, I went to sit in the graveyard. I was looking out at the dark, flat②, wild land divided by the black line of the River Thames and listening to the low sound of the sea far away.

"Don't say one word or I'll cut your throat!"

① **mile** /maɪl/ n. 英里（1 英里 = 1.609 344 千米）

② **flat** /flæt/ adj. 水平的；平坦的

1

cried a frightening voice, as a man jumped up from the graves and grabbed① me. He was a very big man. He was wearing all grey clothes, and he had an iron chain on his leg. He looked very tired and very hungry. Never in my whole life had I been so frightened.

"Please! Don't cut my throat, sir!" I begged as he held on to me②.

"What's your name, boy! Answer me quick!" he said, "And show me the way to your house!"

"Pip's my name, sir. And my house is in the village over there."

Then he turned me upside-down③ and shook me. A piece of old bread fell out of my pocket. He quickly ate this, like a dog, and then sat me back on the stone.

"Where are your parents?" he asked.

"Over there, sir," I answered, pointing to their graves.

"What!" he cried in surprise. He was about to

---

① **grab** /græb/ vt. 抢夺；抓（住）。grab at 热切或拼命地企图抓住

② **hold on to sb./sth.** 抓住。例：The man held on to his hat in the wind. 那男子在大风中按住了自己的帽子。

③ **upside-down** adj./adv. 倒转（置）的；[喻] 混乱（的）地

run, but then he saw that I was pointing to their gravestone. "Oh!" he said, more calmly, "I see. They're dead. Then who's taking care of you? Who do you live with, if I let you live, that is?"

"My sister takes care of me, sir. She's the wife of Joe Gargery, the village ironworker."

"Ironworker, you say?" He looked down at his leg. Then he brought me close to his face and looked violently into my eyes.

"Now look here," he said. "You get me a tool to cut this chain off my leg. And also bring me some food. You'd better do this or I'll cut your heart out. If you tell anyone else, I'll come after you just the same."

"I promise I'll do what you ask, sir," I answered. My whole body was shaking from fright①.

"My friend, who's just over there, cooks boys' hearts and eats them. So wherever you are, he'll find you and take your heart out. Bring the tool I need and the food to that wooden building over there by early tomorrow morning. Remember, you promised!"

---

① **fright** /fraɪt/ *n.* 恐怖；惊恐

Then he turned and walked across the wetlands. The chain around his leg made it difficult for him. After he disappeared from sight, I ran home as fast as I could.

My sister, Mrs. Joe Gargery, raised me since I was a little boy. She believed that all children had to be brought up "by hand". Nobody explained to me what "by hand" meant, but my sister was very proud of the fact that she had brought me up "by hand". She had both a hard and a heavy hand, and she used it freely on Joe as well as me. I believed it is safe① to say that Joe and I were both brought up by hand. In other words, my sister brought us up most strictly. In looks she was not a beauty, being much too tall and thin, with black hair and eyes and a very red face. She often complained about Joe and I causing her a world of trouble②, which I guess we did as she always complained about us. Joe, on the other hand, was a gentle and kind man. He had light hair and blue accepting eyes.

Joe and I were good friends because we were in the same position, that is, of being scolded by Mrs.

① **safe** /seɪf/ *adj.* 稳妥的；恰当的。safe and sound 平安无事
② **a world of trouble** 许多麻烦。a world of sth. 大量，许多

Joe. Joe would try to protect me from her anger whenever he could. So later that day when I ran breathless into the kitchen after my meeting with the strange man, he gave me a friendly warning. "She's out trying to find you, Pip! And she has the beating stick with her!" I knew this stick quite well. It had been used so often on me that it was quite smooth by now.

Just then my sister rushed in.

"And where have you been, you monkey①?" she shouted. I hid behind Joe so that she couldn't hit me with the stick.

"Only to the churchyard," I whispered. I almost started to cry.

"Churchyard! If I hadn't decided to bring you up, the churchyard's where you'd be right now— dead with our parents! One day you'll send me to the churchyard!"

For the rest of the evening I couldn't stop thinking about the stranger I had met on the wetlands. When the wind blew outside, I imagined I could hear his voice and the voice of the young man who ate boys'

---

① **monkey** /ˈmʌŋkɪ/ *n.* 口语中指顽皮的儿童、淘气鬼。make a monkey of sb. 愚弄某人

hearts.

Just before going to bed, we heard the sound of a big gun out on the wetlands. "Was that a gun, Joe?" I asked.

"Ah, yes!" said Joe. "It means another prisoner has escaped. I heard that one prisoner managed to escape last night."

"Is it the police that fires the gun?" I asked. I looked at Joe and he shook his head as if to warn① me.

My sister replied by angrily cutting me short②. "Too many questions," she frowned. "If you must know it's those men in the prison-ships who fire the gun."

I really wanted to know more, so I managed to ask in a quiet way, "I wonder who is in prison-ships, and why?"

This questioning of mine was too much for③ Mrs. Joe. "Listen, you! I didn't bring you up by hand to bother people all the time! The river has ships on it that are used as prisons. These places are for thieves and murderers, and they stay on those ships for years sometimes. And when they were little they would ask

---

① **warn** /wɔːn/ *vt.* 警告；告诫
② **cut sb. short** 打断某人的话
③ **be too much for...** 非……力所能及；非……所应付得了

too many questions! Now, go to bed!"

I wasn't able to sleep all night. I was afraid of the young man who would take my heart, I was afraid of the stranger with the iron chain, and I was afraid that my sister would later discover that some food had been stolen. As soon as the sky became a little bright outside my window, I got out of bed and quietly went down to the kitchen. I stole some bread and cheese, and a big meat pie. I was hoping that nobody would notice the food that was missing[①], as there was a lot of food ready for Christmas. I wasn't brave enough to take the whole bottle of wine for that would surely be noticed. So I poured some wine into a smaller bottle and put it in my bag. Then I filled up the big wine bottle with what I thought was water from a big brown bottle. Then I went to Joe's box of tools to find the tool the stranger wanted. When I ran outside, it was still quite dark.

The mist was so thick that I wasn't able to see anything. It was difficult finding my way to the wooden building and I almost got lost. When I was near the building I saw a man sitting on the

---

① **missing** /ˈmɪsɪŋ/ *adj.* 失踪的；找不到的；漏掉的

ground, half asleep. I went up to him and touched his shoulder. He jumped up in surprise and then I realized it was the wrong man! It was another man dressed in grey, and he also had an iron chain on his leg. He quickly took off① into the mist.

"Oh no!" I thought. "It's the young man who eats boys' hearts!" A feeling of pain came into my heart.

When I reached the building, I saw the stranger I had met before. He looked so cold and hungry that I even felt sorry for him. Shaking violently, he swallowed the wine and ate the food as quickly as he could. He looked like a hunted animal as he kept looking around all the time for danger.

"Are you sure you didn't tell anyone? Or bring anyone?"

"No sir! I'm glad you like the food, sir."

"Thank you, my boy. You've been kind to a poor man."

"But it looks like you haven't left any for him."

"Him? Who do you mean?" My friend stopped in the middle of eating.

"The young man who travels② with you."

---

① **take off** 匆匆离开。例：He took off for the station at a run. 他匆匆向车站跑去。

② **travel** /ˈtrævl/ *vi.* 此处指"交往"。travel with bad elements 与坏人交往

"Oh, him!" he replied, smiling, "He doesn't want any food."

"I thought he looked pretty hungry when I saw him," I answered.

He opened his eyes wide in great surprise. "Looked? When?" he asked.

"Just now, over there in the churchyard. I thought it was you because he was dressed[①] like you, and I went over and woke him up and—" I was anxious to express this as politely as I could "—it looked like he had the same reason for wanting to borrow this tool I brought."

"Then I did hear the gun being fired last night! You know, boy, when you're alone at night, you imagine all kinds of things—voices calling, guns firing, soldiers marching! But tell me where this man went. When I find him I'll smash[②] his face and be finished with him[③]! Let me have the tool first."

I became afraid of him again now that he was angry.

---

① 注意 **dress** 与 put on，wear 的区别。［辨］按穿的动作或状态区分：put on 表穿的动作；wear 表穿着的状态；dress 依据搭配既可表动作又可表状态；be dressed in 表状态。

② **smash** /smæʃ/ *vt.* 打成粉碎；击败。smash the enemy 击溃敌人

③ **finish with sb./sth.** 与……断绝关系，终止与某物联系

"I'm sorry," I apologized, "I have to go home now." He paid no further attention to me and was bending over his chained leg, cutting away at^① the iron like a crazy man. I ran as fast as I can towards home. When I stopped halfway home in the mist, I could still hear the sound of him trying to cut his chain.

---

① **cut away at** 试图用刀等截断、破开某物

Chapter 2
After a Prisoner

I was frightened all morning that my sister would discover the stolen food, but she was so busy cleaning the house and roasting chickens for Christmas lunch that she did not even notice I had been away, or that anything was missing. Our guests arrived at half past one. The first to arrive was Mr. Wopsle, who had a large nose and a shining, bald[1] forehead. He was the church clerk. Mr. Pumblechook, the shopkeeper, arrived next. He was a fat, middle-aged man with a mouth like a fish, and staring eyes. He was Joe's uncle but it was only Mrs. Joe who called him uncle. He arrived with two bottles of wine, just like he did every Christmas, and handed them proudly to my sister.

"Oh Uncle Pumblechook! This is so kind of you!" she always replied.

"No more than you deserve," was his answer every time.

---

① **bald** /bɔːld/ *adj.* 秃头的

11

I would have felt uncomfortable with these guests even if I wasn't worried about stealing food from① my sister. Pumblechook's elbow was in my eye②, I wasn't allowed to say a single word, and they gave me the worst pieces of meat. These parts of their bodies even the chickens must have been ashamed of when they were alive. Worse than all of this was the constant bothering by the company.

"Before we eat, let us give thanks to God for the food③ in front of us," said Mr. Wopsle, in the same deep voice he used in church.

Just to make me feel worse, my sister whispered, "Do you hear that? Be grateful!"

Mr. Pumblechook added, "be grateful, boy, especially to those who brought you up by hand."

"Why are the young never grateful?" asked Mr. Wopsle, as if the young made him feel sad.

"The characters of young children are naturally bad," answered Mr. Pumblechook. Then all three

---

① **steal food from...** 表示"偷，抢，骗"的三个近义词的不同搭配为：rob (抢) sb. of sth. 抢 (夺) 某人某物；steal (偷) sth. from sb. 偷某人某物；cheat (骗) sb. (out) of sth. 骗某人某物。

② **Pumblechook's elbow was in my eye** 指矮小的匹浦被这群大人们挤着坐着，在餐桌上几乎无一席之地。

③ **let us... for the food** 按照传统的西方风俗，一些西方家庭尤其是信仰基督教的家庭在开始吃饭前，往往要低头做简短的祷告，感谢上帝赐予他们食物。

looked at me.

When guests were at our house, Joe's position was even lower than usual (if that was possible). Still, he always tried to help me and make me feel better. Sometimes he helped me by giving me extra sauce①. He did that now.

"Just imagine your life, boy," said Mr. Pumblechook, "if your sister hadn't raised you—"

"You better listen," added my sister angrily.

"If, as I say, she hadn't given her life and happiness looking after you, where would you be now?"

Joe gave me more sauce.

"We know how troublesome he was to you, madam," Mr. Wopsle understandingly added.

"Trouble?" she cried. "Trouble?!" Then she began to list all my illnesses, accidents② and crimes③, while her two guests looked at me with fright and disgust④.⑤ Joe added more sauce to the meat on my plate even though my plate was completely covered in sauce, and

---

① **sauce** /sɔ:s/ *n.* 沙司；酱；调味汁

② **accident** /ˈæksɪdənt/ *n.* 事故；机遇

③ **crime** /kraɪm/ *n.* 罪行，犯罪

④ **disgust** /dɪsˈɡʌst/ *n.* 反感，厌恶

⑤ **Then she began to list... and disgust.** 作者用这些语言描绘 Pip 姐姐怎样夸大 Pip 所带来的麻烦，以表明自己照顾 Pip 的辛苦与功劳。

I wanted to pull Mr. Wopsle's nose.

Finally Mrs. Joe stopped for breath and said to Mr. Pumblechook, "Have a little wine, uncle. I already have a bottle open."

It was going to happen at last! Now there was no hiding the fact that I had stolen some wine, and put water in the bottle. Before drinking Mr. Pumblechook held the wine up to the light, smiled importantly[①] at his glass and drank it. Almost immediately he jumped up and rushed around the room in a strange wild dance. Everyone looked hard at him in great surprise. Was he crazy? I wondered if I might have poisoned him. He fell backwards into a chair, crying "Medicine!" Then I understood what I had done. Instead of filling up the bottle with water, I had accidentally[②] put Mrs. Joe's strongest and most unpleasant medicine! That was what was in the big brown bottle.

"But how on earth did my medicine get into that wine bottle?" asked my sister. Luckily for me she had to get poor Mr. Pumblechook some hot

---

① **importantly** /ɪmˈpɔːtəntlɪ/ *adv.* 神气十足地；得意扬扬地

② **accidentally** /ˌæksɪˈdentəlɪ/ *adv.* 意外（偶然）地。accidentally = by accident = by chance 偶然

rum① to get rid of the medicine's taste. "And now," she said, once the fat man became somewhat calmer, "you must all try Uncle Pumblechook's present of a really delicious meat pie!"

"That's right, Mrs. Joe!" agreed Mr. Pumblechook. "A tastier pie you will not find!" I was glad that his pride made him quickly forget the medicine.

"You shall eat some as well, Pip," said Joe kindly.

I knew what was going to happen next. I jumped down from the table, and ran out of the room.

I got as far as the front door when I ran straight into a group of soldiers. As I was standing there Mrs. Joe came out of the kitchen saying, "The pie—has gone!" Then she stopped when she saw the soldiers.

"Excuse me for disturbing you on this fine day, ladies and gentlemen," said the officer in charge. "I'm here in the name of the King②, and I want the ironworker."

"Why do you want him?" said my sister angrily.

The officer must have thought it a good idea to first calm Mrs. Joe. "Madam," he replied politely, "speaking for myself, I'd like to have the pleasure

---

① **rum** /rʌm/ *n.* 朗姆酒，用甘蔗汁蒸馏制成的糖酒

② **in the name of sb./sth.** 代表某人（某物）

of meeting his fine wife. But the King would like him to repair these." The officer gave Joe a pair of handcuffs① for prisoners.

"Ah, very good, very good!" said Mr. Pumble-chook, for no particular reason.

The soldiers decided to wait in the kitchen while Joe made the fire ready for work. I was feeling much better now that everyone had forgotten the missing pie.

"How far are the wetlands from us?" asked the officer.

"About one mile," replied Mrs. Joe.

"That's good. We'll catch those prisoners before dark."

"Prisoners, officer?" asked Mr. Wopsle.

"Yes, two escaped prisoners out on the wetlands. Any sign of them?"

The others all shook their heads and thankfully, no one bothered② to ask me. When the handcuffs were repaired, Joe suggested we go with the soldiers to help them. Mrs. Joe was curious to know what happened so she agreed to let us go. So Joe,

---

① **handcuff** /ˈhændkʌf/ *n.* 手铐

② **bother** /ˈbɒðə/ *vt.* 打扰

Mr. Wopsle and I followed the soldiers out onto the wetlands.

"I hope we don't find any prisoners, Joe," I whispered.

"I hope not too, Pip," he whispered back. It was starting to get dark and a cold, east wind was blowing from the sea.

Suddenly we heard shouts in the distance.

"This way! Quickly!" ordered the officer, and we all ran in that direction①. The shouts became clearer and louder. "Murder!" "Escaped prisoners!" "Help!" At last we saw two men in the distance fighting one another. One was the prisoner I had helped, and the other was the man who ran away from me when I woke him up near the wooden building. Somehow the soldiers managed to break the men apart and put the handcuffs on them.

"Here he is, the murderer. I'm holding him for you!" shouted my prisoner.

"Officer, he tried to murder me!" shouted the other man. His face was cut and he was bleeding.

"Murder him! No," said my prisoner, "that

---

① **in that direction** 朝某方向去

would be too easy. I want him to suffer back on the prison-ship. He's a liar, and he lied[①] at our trial! You can't trust Compeyson!"

Then he noticed me standing with the soldiers. I shook my head at him to let him know I hadn't told the soldiers about him. He just looked hard at me, and I was unsure whether he would say anything or not.

The prisoners were taken by the soldiers to the river bank. There was a boat there waiting to take them back to the prison-ship. Just as he was getting into the boat, my prisoner said, "Officer, after I escaped I stole some food from the ironworker's house. Bread, cheese, wine and a meat pie. I'm sorry I ate your pie, ironworker."

"I'm glad you did," replied Joe. He was so kind of heart. "We wouldn't want you dying of hunger, even if you are a prisoner."

The prisoner looked deeply touched by Joe's words and rubbed his eyes with the back of his hand. We watched him until he boarded[②] the prison-ship and disappeared. I thought that would be the last I would ever see of him.

① **lie** /laɪ/ *vi.* 说谎（规则动词：lied，lied），此意的名词形式为 liar（说谎的人）
② **board** /bɔːd/ *vt.* 上（船、火车、飞机等）board the plane 上飞机

19

Chapter 3
A Good Chance for Pip

I always knew I would serve under and be taught by Joe as soon as I was old enough, and so I used to spend most of the day helping him in the iron workshop. However, I also attended the village evening school, which was organized by an ancient relation① of Mr. Wopsle's. Her teaching mostly consisted of falling asleep while we children fought each other, but Mr. Wopsle's young cousin, Biddy, tried to keep us under control and teach us to read, write and count. Mr. Wopsle would come every three months and give us an examination. The truth is he never asked us any questions at all, but read Shakespeare to us, playing the roles and enjoying the sound of his own voice.

One night, almost a year after the event with the escaped prisoners, I was sitting by the kitchen fire writing a letter to Joe. There wasn't any need for me to write him a letter because he was sitting

---

① **relation** /rɪˈleɪʃən/ n. 关系，联系；亲属

right next to me, but I wanted to practice my writing. After working hard for an hour or two, I gave this letter to him.

"My dear Joe I hope you are well soon I can teach you what I have learnt what fun Joe love Pip."

"Pip, my boy!" cried Joe. He opened his kind blue eyes very wide and shouted, "What a lot of wonderful things you've learnt! Here's a 'J' and an 'O', that's for 'Joe', isn't it, Pip?"

"How do you write Gargery, Joe?"

"I don't know much about writing," said Joe. "But, you know, I like reading. Give me a good book or newspaper, a good fire and I'm happy. Well! When you can find a 'J' and an 'O', how interesting reading is[①]!"

"Did you go to school, Joe, when you were young?"

"No, Pip. You see, there wasn't a chance for me to go to school. My father wasn't the nicest of men and he used to drink a lot. Sometimes my mother and I would run away from him and she'd always say, 'Joe, now you can go to school.' But my father

---

① **When you can... is** 这句话描写了乔不识字，但又很要面子，不愿意承认自己是文盲。这表现了作者的幽默感，但并没有损害乔的形象，只是突出了他孩子般的幼稚和单纯。

had such love for us he couldn't be without us. He always came to find us, and took us home, and hit us. So you see, Pip, I never learnt much."

"That's terrible! Poor Joe!"

"But remember, Pip, my father had a good heart and a lot of love."

I wondered whether that was true, but I didn't say anything to Joe.

"He let me become an ironworker, which was his job too, you know. But he never worked much and I earned the money for the family until he died. And listen to this, Pip. I wanted to put these words above his grave:

Whatever the fault he had from the start,

Remember, reader, he had a good heart."

"Did you make that up① yourself, Joe?" I asked, surprised.

"I certainly did," answered Joe proudly. "But Pip, sad to say, we couldn't buy a gravestone. My poor mother needed money as she was in bad health. She died soon after and found her peace② at last." I looked at Joe and could see tears in his

---

① **make sth. up** 虚构、编造某事
② **found her peace** peace 本指和平、和睦、安宁，但此处是 die（死）的委婉语。

blue eyes. "I was really lonely then, and I met your sister. Now look here, Pip," said Joe, looking straight at me, because he knew I had different thoughts. "Your sister is a fine woman!" he said.

I could say nothing better than "I'm glad you think so, Joe."

"So am I," said Joe. "I'm glad I think so. So very kind of her to bring you up by hand. And what a tiny baby you were! When I offered to marry your sister, I said to her, 'And bring the poor little child to live with us. We'll make room for him at the iron workshop!'" I jumped up and put my arms round Joe's neck, crying into his shirt.

"There now! Don't cry, old boy!" he said. "We'll always be the best of friends, you and me!" "So here we are, Pip! Now if you teach me a little (and I warn you now that I'm very stupid) Mrs. Joe must never find out. Why? Because she likes to be—in charge—you know—giving the orders."

"Joe," I asked him, "why don't you ever stand up to her[①] and fight for yourself?"

"Well," said Joe, "your sister's really clever and

---

① **stand up to sb.** 对抗某人

I'm not. And another thing, and this is serious, old boy, I think of the hard life my poor mother had and I promised myself I would always behave right to a woman. I'd much rather seem a bit weak or foolish than fight or hit her. I feel badly that she treats you the way she does. I wish I could take all the scolding myself. But there it is, Pip."

Just then we heard Mrs. Joe and Uncle Pumblechook returning from the market. The carriage stopped and soon, in a rush of cold air, they came into the kitchen.

"Now if this boy isn't thankful tonight, he never will be!" Mrs. Joe shouted at me.

"What a great opportunity she's giving the boy," agreed Pumblechook. I tried to look grateful and looked at Joe, making the word "She?" silently with my lips. Joe clearly did not know what was going on either.

"Did you say 'she'?" he asked politely.

"She is a she, I suppose," Mrs. Joe replied impatiently. "Unless you think Miss Havisham could be a 'he'. And even you wouldn't do that."

"Do you mean the rich Miss Havisham who lives all alone in the big house in town?" asked Joe.

"Do you know any other Miss Havishams?! She wants the boy to go and play there at her house. She asked Uncle Pumblechook if he knew of[1] any young boys. And Uncle Pumblechook, taking care of us as he always does, suggested Pip. What's even better is, as Uncle Pumblechook so cleverly knows, this boy's fortune may be made! Our kind uncle has offered to take him into town tonight in his carriage, putting him up[2] for the night to deliver him tomorrow to Miss Havisham's. And look!" she cried, pointing her finger at me. "Look at how dirty he is!"

Mrs. Joe washed me from head to toe in her usual violent manner, and handed me over in my tightest Sunday clothes[3] to Mr. Pumblechook. I cried a little riding into town because I had never been away from Joe before, and I had no idea what was going to happen to me at Miss Havisham's.

Mr. Pumblechook's thoughts about children were the same as my sister's, and so for breakfast the next morning he gave me a large piece of bread

---

① **know of** 知道某人的情况

② **put sb. up** 向某人提供食宿

③ **Sunday clothes** 多指（自己衣服中）最好的衣服

with very little butter, followed by a cup of warm water with very little milk. Then he demanded to test my math.

"What's seven and thirteen, boy?" All through breakfast he continued testing me. "And nine? And eleven?"

I was actually glad to arrive at Miss Havisham's house at about ten o'clock. It was a large house made of old stone, and there were iron bars on the windows. Even at the gate Mr. Pumblechook continued to test me. "And fourteen?" he asked. But I pretended not to hear him. Then a young lady came to open the gate. Mr. Pumblechook was following me through the gate when she stopped him.

"Do you wish to see Miss Havisham as well?" she asked.

"If Miss Havisham wishes to see me," answered Mr. Pumblechook, a little confused.

"Ah!" said the girl, "she doesn't."

Mr. Pumblechook was shocked but dared not disobey Miss Havisham's wishes. Before leaving he whispered angrily to me, saying "Boy! Remember those who brought you up by hand and behave①

① **behave** /bɪˈheɪv/ *vi.* 举动，表现；*vt.* 使表现好

well!" I expected him to call through the gate, "And sixteen?" but he did not.

The garden leading to the house looked like it hadn't been kept in ages①. The young lady leading me through the garden was not very friendly, either. She was the same age as me, but kept calling me "boy". To me she seemed much older than her age. She was as beautiful and as proud as a queen. After going through many dark passages we reached a door, where she left me, outside, taking her candle with her.

I knocked at the door and was told to enter. I was in the middle of a large dark room where the curtains were shut. A hundred candles lit the room. In the middle of the room, sitting at a table, was the strangest lady I have ever seen, or shall ever see. Wearing a wedding dress made of rich material, she still had wedding flowers in her hair, but her hair was all white from age. Around her were suitcases of dresses and jewels, as if she was getting ready to go for a trip. She also had only one white shoe on. I realized that the white wedding dress had become

---

① **keep in ages** 1) keep 此处为 "整理，料理"；2) age 本指年龄，若是复数形式在口语中多指 "很长一段时间"。

yellow with age, and that the flowers in her hair had all died, and that the bride inside the dress had grown old. The room and everything in it was old and dying. Her dark eyes seemed the only thing alive in the room.

"Who are you?" said the strange lady.

"Pip, madam. Mr. Pumblechook's boy. I've come here—to play."

"Come closer and let me look at you." Standing in front of her, I saw that both her watch and a clock in the room had stopped at twenty minutes to nine.

"Are you afraid of an old woman who has never seen the sun since you were born?" asked Miss Havisham.

Though I knew it was a lie I said, "No."

Putting her hand on her left side, she asked, "Do you know what this is?"

All of a sudden I remembered my prisoner's traveling companion. "That's your heart, madam," I answered.

"My heart! Broken!" she cried with a strange, proud smile. Then she said, "I am tired and need something different. Play for me."

No request could have been more difficult to obey in that house and that room. I just stood there helplessly.

"I'm very sorry, madam," I said, "Even though I know my sister will be very angry[①] with me if you complain, I can't play just now. This place is so strange, and new, and sad..." I stopped, afraid of making Miss Havisham angry. Then she looked down at her dress, and then at herself in the mirror on the table.

"So strange to him, so well-known to me," she whispered as if forgetting I was there. "So new to him, so old to me. And so sad to us both! Call Estella!"

Estella finally came in with her candle. Miss Havisham picked up a jewel that was on her table and put it in Estella's hair. "You look very pretty, my darling. One day it will be yours. Now let me watch you play cards with this boy."

"With him! He's a common working boy!" she cried.

Then I heard Miss Havisham whisper, "So be

---

① **angry** /ˈæŋgrɪ/ adj. 愤怒的；生气的。be angry with sb. 生某人的气；be angry at/about sth. 因某事而生气

it! You can break his heart, anyway!" She sat by her table as if she were already dead and watched us play cards in the candlelight. I began to wonder if daylight would turn her into dust.

"What ugly and rough[①] hands this boy has! And look at his thick boots!" cried Estella before we had finished our first game. I became ashamed because I knew what she said was true.

"And what do you think of her?" whispered Miss Havisham to me.

"She's very proud," I whispered back.

"Anything else?"

"I think she's very pretty."

"Anything else?"

"She's not polite. And—and I'd like to go home now."

"And never see her again, even though she's so very pretty?"

"I, I'd—I'd like to go home now."

My answer finally made Miss Havisham smile. "You can go home. Come again in six days' time. Estella, give him some food to eat. You can go, Pip."

---

① **rough** /rʌf/ *adj.* 粗糙（略）的；参差不齐的；粗鲁（野）的；剧烈的

And so I found myself back in the overgrown[①] garden in the bright daylight. Estella put some bread and meat down on the ground for me, like I was a dog. I was so upset by the way she treated me that I started to cry. As soon as she saw this, she started to laugh, and pushed me out of the gate. I walked the four miles home to the iron workshop, thinking about all I had seen at that strange house. Looking at my hands and boots made me sad, and I knew that I was only a common working boy and wished to be different.

My sister wouldn't stop asking me questions. She wanted to know all the details of my visit. Because it was so strange and also because I felt I did not want to, I couldn't explain what happened at Miss Havisham's or her strange house. I knew my sister would not understand. Worst of all old fool Pumblechook arrived around tea time to ask me more questions. His staring eyes and open mouth reminded me of a fish[②] and made me want to keep silent.

"Let me try to make this boy speak, madam," he told Mrs. Joe. "I'll make him answer our questions.

① **overgrown** /ˌəʊvəˈɡrəʊn/ *adj.* 杂草丛生的。固定搭配：overgrown with sth.

② **remind sb. of sth.** 使某人想起某事

Now, boy, what's forty-three and seventy-two?"

"I don't know," I replied. I didn't care, either.

Trying to be funny, he jokingly said, "Is it eighty-five, for example?"

"Yes!" I answered, even though I knew it wasn't. For that answer my sister hit me hard on the head①.

"Boy!" he yelled. "Tell us about Miss Havisham."

Even though I knew it was wrong, I decided to lie. "Very tall and dark," I said.

"Is she, uncle?" asked my curious sister.

"Oh yes," answered Mr. Pumblechook. Then I knew immediately that he had never seen her before. "This is how to get information from this boy," he added with authority to Mrs. Joe.

"How wonderful you make him obey you, uncle!" said Mrs. Joe.

"Now, boy!" he began again, "what was Miss Havisham doing when you arrived?"

"She was sitting inside a huge black box that was in the living room," I replied.

Mr. Pumblechook and Mrs. Joe looked hard at each other. "In a black box?" they repeated.

---

① **hit me hard on the head** 打某人身体某部位。结构：hit sb.+ 介词 + 身体部位。

"Yes," I said. I started to become more confident. "And Miss Estella, who is her niece, I think, was giving her gold plates with cake and wine through little windows that were in the box."

"Was there anybody else in the living room?" asked Mr. Pumblechook.

"Four dogs, and they were huge. They were eating meat out of a silver basket."

"Can this be possible, uncle?" asked Mrs. Joe.

"I know she's a strange woman, madam. It's certainly possible. What did you play at[①], boy?"

"We played with flags," I answered, surprised at the lies I was telling. "Estella had a blue one, and I was given a red one, and Miss Havisham had a flag with little gold stars on it that she stuck out of a window of that huge black box."

Fortunately they didn't ask me any more questions. They were still talking about all the wonderful things I had seen when Joe came into the room. They repeated what I had said and I saw his blue eyes open wide in surprise. This made me feel very sorry that I had lied. Later that evening, as soon as

---

① **play at** 做（游戏）；打（球、牌等）；下（棋）；参加（比赛）

I was alone with Joe for a moment, I told him that I had lied about my visit to Miss Havisham's.

"None of it is true, Pip?" he asked, surprised. "No huge black box? There were dogs, though, weren't there, Pip? No? Not even one dog?"

"No, Joe, I'm sorry I lied."

His kind face looked very unhappy and he said, "Pip dear boy! If you tell lies, what will happen to you when you die①?"

"I know, Joe, it's terrible to lie, but I couldn't help myself. Today a beautiful young lady at Miss Havisham's said I was common because of my thick boots and rough hands. And I know I am! I feel so miserable and somehow I thought I'd feel better if I told some lies."

"Oh, Pip," said Joe, lighting his pipe slowly, "you can't stop being common by telling lies. Lies are wrong and can never make you any better. And remember you're learning all the time, Pip! Just think of that letter you wrote me last night! All the rich people, even the King, they had to start their learning from the beginning, too, isn't that right? So

---

① **If you tell lies, ...die?** 此句渗透了西方人的宗教思想，他们认为，人若在生前说谎或干坏事而无悔意，死后则要下地狱以接受上帝的惩罚。

I guess no flags at Miss Havisham's? That's a pity. Look here, Pip, as a true friend speaking to you, take my advice and remember, 'No more lies, live well, and die happy.'"

Joe's honest words made me feel better and I went to bed, but I couldn't stop myself thinking about Estella and how she would think that Joe's boots were also too thick and his hands also too coarse[1]. I knew that she would consider our whole family common. From that night on, I decided never to work in the iron workshop.

---

[1] **coarse** /kɔːs/ *adj.* 粗糙（鲁）的，它往往指本质不够精巧，也含有 "不文雅" 之意。

Chapter 4
A Present from a Stranger

I wanted to be accepted by Estella so badly that I even asked Mr. Wopsle's cousin Biddy to begin teaching me everything she knew. Even though she helped me the best she could, I knew it would be a long time before I could reach Estella's level of education.

One evening I went to the village pub to fetch Joe. Though she never allowed him much, my sister would sometimes allow Joe a trip to the pub to smoke his pipe and have a beer. When I arrived Mr. Wopsle and Joe were sitting with a man I'd never seen before. He wore a big hat that covered most of his head, and one of his eyes was half-closed. He had just ordered hot rum for the three of them, and looked very interestedly at me when I arrived.

"I find it very lonely out here in the country, gentlemen," he said.

"Yes," said Joe, "just wetlands as far as one can see, all the way① down to the river."

① **all the way** 从头至尾；自始至终，一直

37

"Do people ever spend the night on the wetlands?" asked the stranger.

"No," replied Joe, "except an escaped prisoner now and then. They can hide quite well there. One night all of us went out to look for one, didn't we, Pip?"

"Yes, that's right, Joe."

The stranger looked at me with his good eye.

"His name is Pip? Is he your son?"

"He's the wife's brother," explained Mr. Wopsle, sounding very official① in his church clerk's voice.

The drinks arrived, and the stranger began to mix his hot rum and water not with a spoon, but with a tool for cutting iron. He put the tool back in his pocket when he had finished, but not before he looked at me to make sure that I had seen it, too. As soon as I saw the tool, I knew it was the one I had stolen from Joe, and I knew that this man knew my prisoner. I looked at him in horror.

The men continued to speak to one another in a friendly way until Joe stood up. He took my hand to leave.

"Please, a moment," said the stranger. "I want

---

① **official** /əˈfɪʃəl/ adj. 正式的；官方的

to give the boy something." He wrapped① a gold coin in some old paper from his pocket and handed it to me with a look full of meaning. "That's yours!" he said.

"Thank you, sir," I said, even though I could hardly talk after knowing who it was. Joe and I walked home together and Joe kept his mouth open all the way home so that my sister wouldn't know that he had been drinking rum.

When we arrived home, we took out the coin from the paper and found two pounds that the stranger had given me as well. My sister thought the stranger must have made a mistake, so she kept the pound notes② in case he came back. I didn't feel good about the two pounds. I knew they were from my prisoner, and I felt having such criminal friends made me more common than ever.

The next time I went to Miss Havisham's house, I had to wait in a different room. There were several ladies and gentlemen, relations of hers, who were waiting as well. Estella called my name first to enter and her relatives turned and looked at me in

---

① **wrap** /ræp/ vt. 包，裹
② **note** /nəʊt/ *n.* 此处指纸币

disgust.

Leading me along the dark passages, Estella looked more beautiful than the first time I saw her. She stopped suddenly and put her face close to mine.

"Look at me, common boy! Do you think I am pretty?"

"Yes, you're very pretty."

"Am I rude to you?"

"Not as rude as last time."

Then she slapped① my face very hard.

"You rough, common little boy! Now what do you think of me?"

"I won't tell you."

"Are you going to cry again, you fool?"

"I'll never cry for you again," I said. I knew this was a lie, because I was crying inside after she slapped me, and only I would know later how much I cried for her.

As we made our way② upstairs we met a gentleman. He was a large, heavy man, with very dark skin, sharp eyes, and a huge head that had

---

① **slap** /slæp/ vt. (用扁平东西等) 捆; 拍; 掌击
② **make one's way** 前进; 行进

little hair. He smelled strongly of perfumed soap. At the time I didn't know how important he would become later in my life.

"Who's this?" he asked Estella, stopping to look at me.

"A local boy. Miss Havisham asked for him," she replied.

"Well, I think most boys are bad," he said to me. "So you'd better behave yourself!" He continued downstairs in the dark.

This time Miss Havisham was in a room I had not seen before. The furniture was completely covered in dust. In the middle of the room was a long table, and in the middle of the table was a large yellow thing, with hundreds of insects running around it. I felt quite sick[①] looking at the insects.

"This table," said Miss Havisham, "is where they will lay me after I'm dead. Here my relations can come and look at me." She laid her bony hand on my shoulder, but I didn't want her to touch me. I thought she was going to die there and then. "That," she added, pointing to the yellow shape, "was my

---

① **sick** /sɪk/ *adj.* 可作表语或定语，表示：1) 有病的；2) 恶心的。

wedding cake. My wedding cake!" she shouted. "Come!" she suddenly said. "Call Estella and help me walk round the room!"

I had to hold her arm to help her as she walked. As we were going slowly and around the room, Estella brought in Miss Havisham's relations. They had been waiting downstairs for a long time. As they stood watching us at the door, I began to feel that they blamed me for Miss Havisham's cold manner towards them.

"Dear Miss Havisham!" said one of the ladies, trying to sound caring. "How well you look in your dress!"

"You know I do not," replied Miss Havisham sharply. "I am nothing but yellow skin and bone."

"It's not possible for Miss Havisham to look well after all her suffering," said a second lady[1] quickly. "An impossible and silly idea!"

"And how are you doing?" Miss Havisham asked this lady. We were close to her then and I would have stopped, but Miss Havisham insisted on walking past her. I thought it was a rather rude way

---

① **a second lady** a+ 序数词 + 名词：又一个，再一个。

to treat guests.

"Not well," said this lady sadly. "My feelings are not so important—I often stay awake at night thinking of you and how you are, dear Miss Havisham!"

"Well, you shouldn't!" said Miss Havisham cruelly, and we hurried past the little group again.

"There's nothing I can do. I try to be less sensitive① and loving. But that's how I am and I have to live with myself!" She started to cry softly. "And what of poor Matthew now!" she added. "Matthew never comes to see you, my dear Miss Havisham. But I—"

Upon hearing Matthew's name, Miss Havisham came to a stop in front of the speaker, who suddenly became silent.

"Matthew will be here," said Miss Havisham firmly, "When I die. He will see me laid on that table. All of you will stand around and look at me—you here, you there, you next to her, you two there. So now you know where to stand to look at my dead body. Now leave here, quickly!"

---

① **sensitive** /ˈsensɪtɪv/ *adj.* 易受伤害的；灵敏的；敏感的

The group left slowly from the room. Some were even complaining that they had not spent enough time with their dear relation. After they had all gone, Miss Havisham whispered to me:

"Today is my birthday, Pip. My relations always come on this day once a year to give me their greetings. On this day, long before you were born, I was going to be married. Maybe I shall die on this day too. Then they will lay me in my wedding dress on this table and I'll have my revenge on him①!"

She was a ghostly figure in her yellow-white bride's dress in the heavy, dark room. I felt she had been waiting for death to visit her for a long time. Then she became silent again.

I left the house and was walking towards the gate when something strange happened. I met a pale young gentleman with fair② hair in the garden.

"Hello!" he said. "Come over this way and fight!"

I followed him without a word.

"Wait just a minute," he said, turning round quickly. "First I must give you a reason for fighting.

① **have one's revenge on sb. (for sth.)** 报仇；因某事向某人报仇
② **fair** /feə/ *adj.* （肤色）白皙的；（头发）金色的

There it is!" He pulled my hair and then hit his head hard into my stomach. After this I was ready to fight him, but he kept dancing about so much that I couldn't get close to him.

"Remember to follow the laws of the game!" he said. I thought he knew so much about fighting he would be hard to beat, but I was surprised when I knocked him down to the ground with my first hit. He got up immediately and seemed very glad to be fighting in the correct manner. I knocked him down[1] again with my second hit. Again he got up and I thought him great for his bravery and his cheerfulness. Finally he agreed that I had won, and we said goodbye.

When I reached the gate, I saw that Estella had been waiting for me. I wondered if she had been watching our fight, because she seemed very pleased about something. Before I walked out of the gate she said,

"Here! You can kiss me if you like."

I kissed her cheek. Though I wanted to kiss her so very much, I felt her offer was like a coin

---

[1] **knock sb. down (to)...** 将某人击倒（撞倒）在地上

thrown to a poor common boy, which hurt very much because it was not worth anything.

I continued my visits to Miss Havisham for almost a year. She enjoyed watching my growing love for Estella, but seemed to enjoy more my unhappiness when Estella laughed at me.

"Go ahead, my darling," she whispered in Estella's ear, "break men's hearts and have no mercy[①]! I want my revenge!"

Meanwhile my sister and that old fool Pumble-chook never stopped talking about Miss Havisham and her large wealth, something they expected me to receive part of either before or after her death. One day Miss Havisham decided it was time to have me serve and work under Joe, and ordered me to bring him along to her house. My sister was very angry that she was not invited as well.

Dear Joe simply could not believe his eyes when we entered Miss Havisham's room the next day. The darkness, the candles, the dust, the ancient furniture, the old lady in her bride's dress—it was almost too much for him. He refused to speak

---

① **have no mercy** 毫不留情

to Miss Havisham directly, and spoke only to me during the conversation. I could see Estella laughing at me behind Miss Havisham's shoulder, and I felt deeply embarrassed① by Joe's small intelligence②.

"So," began Miss Havisham, "you are Joe Gargery the ironworker. Are you ready to train Pip as your worker?"

"You know, Pip," replied Joe, speaking to me "that we've both been looking forward to working together. Haven't we, Pip?"

"When he becomes your worker you don't expect any payment?" she continued.

Joe seemed rather hurt and offended by her question. "Between you and me that question doesn't need an answer, does it, Pip?"

Miss Havisham looked kindly at Joe. She was more understanding of his character than Estella. "Here," she said, picking up a little bag from the table, "Pip has earned this. There is twenty-five pound in this bag. Give it to your master Joe, Pip."

Miss Havisham's gift seemed to make Joe go mad. Even so, he insisted on speaking to me.

① **embarrass** /ɪmˈbærəs/ *vt.* 使窘迫（困难）；使麻烦
② **intelligence** /ɪnˈtelɪdʒəns/ *n.* 智力；理解力；聪明

"This is very kind and generous of you, Pip. Very kind. Now, old boy, we must do our duty to each other. Mustn't we, Pip?" I really had no idea what duty Joe was talking about.

"Goodbye, Pip!" said Miss Havisham. "Show them out, Estella!"

"Shall I come again to see you?" I asked on my way out.

"No, Gargery is your master now. Gargery! Remember, this money is because he has been a good boy. Don't expect anything more from me!"

I somehow managed to get Joe out of the house, and in the daylight he slowly returned to normal. In fact, his intelligence was improved because as we walked home he came up with[①] a surprisingly clever plan.

"Well," cried my sister, as soon as we arrived, "you've finished visiting your fine ladies, I suppose? I'm surprised you even bother to come home at all!"

"Miss Havisham wanted me to send," said Joe, as if he couldn't remember the exact words, "her best wishes? Is that right, Pip? To Mrs. J. Gargery..."

---

① **come up with** 提出，后接 a sum of money 意即 "拿出，提供"。

"Best wishes," I agreed.

"Then she apologized for not being in good health enough to..., what was it, Pip?"

"To have the pleasure," I said.

"To have the pleasure of a lady's company," he said, looking like a man glad to pass on a correct message.

This greatly pleased my sister. "She ought to have sent that message earlier, but better late than never. What did she give the boy?"

"Nothing," said Joe firmly. This greatly angered[①] Mrs. Joe and she opened her mouth to start shouting when Joe raised his hand to stop her. "What she gave," he continued, "she gave to his sister, Mrs. J. Gargery. That's what she said. Didn't she, Pip?"

"How much did she give?" asked my sister, laughing. I could not believe she was actually laughing!

"What would you think of ten pounds?" asked Joe.

"Not bad," said my sister.

"Then what would you say to twenty pounds?"

"That's even better!" said my sister.

---

① **anger** /ˈæŋgə/ *vt.* 激怒；使发怒

"Well, here you are—twenty-five pounds, in fact!" said Joe. He delightedly handed the bag to my sister.

Chapter 5
Mrs. Joe Is Attacked

So it was that in a single year everything in my life had changed. I had always wanted to be a worker and student to Joe, and I had always been happy at home, even if I had to put up with my sister's scolding[1]. Now, after going to Miss Havisham's and knowing Estella, I was ashamed of my home and my work and was in fact quite miserable. However, because of Joe, I stayed at the iron workshop and worked my hardest. I never told him how unhappy I was then. I decided the best thing to do was learn to be an ironworker and become an honest, happy, hardworking man. Still, I could not stop thinking about Estella. My greatest fear was that she would one day come to the iron workshop and see my life as a common ironworker, with black face and hands. I knew she would only turn away[2] in disgust.

I continued to study as hard as I could in the

---

① **put up with sb./sth.** 容忍；忍受某人 / 物

② **turn away (from sb./sth.)** 转过脸不面对（不再看着某人 / 物）

evenings. I must admit I did this not to educate myself, but to educate myself for Estella. Likewise, I also tried to educate Joe, not so he would be more educated, but so that I would be less ashamed of him in front of Estella. One Sunday Joe and I went out to study together, as usual, on the wetlands. He never seemed to remember anything from one week to the next. Still, he smoked his pipe comfortably, looking as intelligent as he could. I decided to ask him a question I had been thinking about lately.

"Joe, do you think it would be alright① to visit Miss Havisham again?"

"Well, Pip," said Joe, "she might expect that you've come back expecting her to give you something. She told me she wouldn't give you anything else."

"But, Joe, I've never thanked her, and it's been almost a year since I've been training as an ironworker!"

"True, Pip," said Joe slowly.

"Maybe if you gave me a half day's holiday tomorrow, I could go and visit Miss Est—Havisham."

"Miss Estavisham isn't her name, as far as I know, Pip," said Joe very seriously.

---

① **alright** /ɔːlˈraɪt/ *adj.* 顺利；圆满；无误；等同于 all right

"Please, Joe!"

"All right, Pip, but she may not be happy to see you. If she isn't happy, you'd better not go again."

Joe had another ironworker he could use instead of me. His name was Orlick, and he had no friends or family in the village. He was big and strong, but quite lazy, and he moved about unhurriedly, with his shoulders bent forward and his eyes on the ground. He never liked me, even when I was a child, though I never knew why. When Joe told him about my half-day holiday, he angrily threw down his hammer.

"If young Pip gets a holiday, then I do, too!"

"Well," nodded Joe after thinking for a moment, "I will give you one too."

My sister had been secretly listening to this conversation outside the iron workshop, and she now called to Joe through a window, "You fool! You can't give a holiday to a lazy man like Orlick! If I were his master I'd soon show him!"

"You're just a wicked, ugly, old woman who wants to be everybody's master!" Orlick told her angrily.

"What was that? What did you say?" cried my sister. She began to scream[①]. "Oh! Oh! What did you call me? Someone hold me quick!" Joe and I knew that she was making herself become angrier and angrier. We had seen this happen many times before.

"Hold you!" replied Orlick in disgust. "If you were my wife, I'd hold you tight round the neck until you couldn't breathe!"

"Oh!" screamed my sister. "Me, here as a married woman, being spoken to like this! In my own house! With my husband standing nearby! Oh! Oh![②]" She began to pull her hair loose like a mad woman, and then rushed at the iron workshop door. Luckily, I had locked it.

Poor Joe had no choice but to challenge Orlick to a fight. Since Joe was the strongest man in the village, Orlick was soon, like the pale young gentleman at Miss Havisham's, lying on the ground. Then Joe unlocked the workshop door and picked up my sister, who had also dropped to the ground,

---

① **scream** /skriːm/ vi. 尖声叫喊；大声说话；放声大笑

② **Me, here as... Oh! Oh!** 按照西方国家的社会习俗，男人在结婚时，要宣誓保护自己的妻子不受伤害。因此匹浦姐姐有意说出此番话，以激怒丈夫为其撑腰。

but only after watching the fight through the window. He put her in the kitchen, where she stayed for the rest of the day, while Joe and Orlick shared a glass of beer peacefully together in the iron workshop.

That afternoon I arrived at Miss Havisham's house hoping to see Estella. But it wasn't Estella who opened the gate, just a cousin of the old lady's. Miss Havisham was still looking the same as before.

"Well?" she said, not even asking after me. "I hope you don't expect me to give you anything."

"No, indeed, Miss Havisham. I've only come to express my gratitude① to you for helping me become Joe's worker and student."

"Good. You may come and see me again on your birthday. Ah!" she suddenly cried, "you're looking for Estella, aren't you? Answer me!"

"Ye—yes," I admitted. "Is Miss Estella well?"

"She's gone abroad to receive a lady's education. She's even more beautiful, and she has dozen of admirers. Do you feel you've lost her?" She was laughing so unpleasantly with these last words that I couldn't say anything. She had seen into my heart

---

① **gratitude** /ˈɡrætɪtjuːd/ *n.* 感激，感谢。其形容词为 grateful（感谢的）。

and I left the house feeling even more miserable than before I arrived.

I met Mr. Wopsle on my way through town, and we started the long walk home to the village. It was such a dark, wet, misty night that we barely saw someone ahead of us.

"Hello!" we called out. "Is that Orlick?"

"Yes!" he answered. "I'll join you on the walk home. I've been in town all afternoon, I have. Did you hear the big gun firing from the prison-ships? There must be some prisoners who've escaped." We didn't talk any more, but walked along in silence. We heard the gun firing several times, and I kept thinking about my prisoner.

We arrived at the village very late, and we were surprised to see lights on at the pub. Mr. Wopsle went in to see if something was happening. He came rushing out after a few minutes, shouting, "Something's wrong up at the iron workshop, Pip! Run! They think an escaped prisoner got into the house while Joe was out. Mrs. Joe's been attacked!"

We ran all the way until we reached the iron workshop. In the kitchen was a doctor, Joe, and a group of women. And in the middle of them all, on the floor, was my sister, lying unconscious. She would never yell at us① again.

When Joe arrived home just before ten from the pub, he found Mrs. Joe lying on the floor. She had been hit very hard on the back of the head with a heavy weapon. Beside her on the floor was a prisoner's iron chain. Nothing had been stolen from the house.

The police spent the next week looking into the attack②, but they did not arrest anybody. I thought that the iron chain looked like the one that belonged to my prisoner, but I could not believe that he would attack my sister. That left only Orlick, or the stranger who had shown me the file in the pub many nights ago. But several people had seen Orlick in town all that evening and my only reason for suspecting③ him was the argument he had earlier with my sister. But my sister had argued with everyone in the village at least ten thousand times, so Orlick was not the only suspect. If it

---

① **yell at sb. (about/for sth.)** 叫喊着说（某事）

② **look into sth.** 调查或观察某物

③ **suspect** /səˈspekt/ *vt.* 怀疑；不信任。suspect sb. of (doing) sth. 怀疑某人有某罪

was the stranger who had come to ask for his two pounds back, my sister would have gladly given it to him. I did not know who her attacker could be.

She was ill in bed for quite a long time. Because she could not speak or understand much, her character changed greatly. She became patient and grateful for all everything we did. Not being able to speak, she used to write a word or draw a picture when she wanted something. As she needed someone to take care of her all the time, Biddy came to live with us. She seemed to have a gift for understanding my sister, and she also looked after us all very well.

One day my sister drew a large "T". I brought her toast[①], and tea, but Biddy knew immediately what she wanted.

"That's not a T; it's Orlick's hammer!" she cried. "She wants to see Orlick, though she's forgotten his name!"

I almost expected my sister to accuse Orlick of[②] attacking her, but instead she seemed very happy to see him. After that she would often ask for

① **toast** /təust/ *n.* 吐司；烤面包片；祝酒词
② **accuse sb. of...** 指控某人（做某事）

60

him, and nobody was able to figure out① why.

One Sunday I asked Biddy to come for a walk on the wetlands.

"Biddy," I said quite seriously, "promise you won't tell anyone this. I'm going to tell you a secret. I want to be a gentleman."

"Aren't you happy as you are?" she replied.

I often wondered about this myself, but I didn't want Biddy to say it. "It's a shame, I know," I said. "if I could have been happy working at the iron workshop, it would have been better for all. Perhaps we would have spent more time together. I would have been good enough for you, wouldn't I, Biddy?"

"Oh yes," she said sadly. "But remember I don't ask for very much."

I continued somewhat angrily. "If nobody had told me I was rough and common, I wouldn't have ever known!"

Biddy looked at me. "Well, that's not true or polite. Who said it?"

"A beautiful young lady at Miss Havisham's whom I greatly admire." Before I could stop myself

---

① **figure (sb./sth.) out** 理解；弄明白

I said, "I want to be a gentleman for her!"

"She may not be worth the trouble, Pip," Biddy added gently.

"That may be true, but I can't help myself."

Being the most sensible of girls, Biddy did not try to change my mind. As we walked home, I felt rested and comforted.

"Pip, what a fool you are!" I said to myself. I realized then that I would always be much happier with Biddy than with Estella.

"I wish I could make myself fall in love with you①, Biddy!" I said suddenly. "Do you mind that I speak so openly, as we're such good friends?"

"No, of course not. But you can never fall in love with me, you see," she answered in a quiet, sad voice.

I thought about if I should continue to work with Joe in a common, honest way of life, and perhaps marry② Biddy. Or did I dare to hope that Miss Havisham would give me her fortune and marry me to Estella?

---

① **fall in love with sb.** 爱上某人

② **marry** /ˈmærɪ/ *vt.* 与某人结婚

Chapter 6
Great Expectations

One Saturday evening, when I had been a worker and student to Joe for four years, we were sitting in the pub with other villagers, listening to Mr. Wopsle, when a stranger came and stood in front of our little group.

"I'm looking for the ironworker, Joe Gargery," he said, "and his worker and student, Pip." I knew immediately that he was the gentleman I had met on the stairs when visiting Miss Havisham. However, he didn't recognize me. I could even smell the same perfumed soap on his large hands. "I'd like to have a word with you① two in private," he said to us, so Joe and I left the pub and walked home with him.

"I'm a lawyer and my name is Jaggers," he said, when he reached the iron workshop. "Joe Gargery, I am sent by someone who suggests ending this boy's worker and studentship to you. Would you want any money to replace him?"

---

① **have a word with sb. (about sth.)** 对某人说（某事）（尤指私下的或秘密的事）

63

"I'd never do anything to stand in Pip's way①," said Joe, staring. "The answer to money is no."

"Remember you can't change that answer later," warned Mr. Jaggers. "Now, remember, I'm just a messenger, I don't speak for myself②, but what I want to say is that this young man has great expectations."

Joe and I were shocked into silence and could only look at each other.

"He will be very rich when he is older. In addition, the person who is taking care of him and whom I work for wants him to leave his home and be educated as a gentleman."

My dream had finally come true. Miss Havisham was going to make me rich!

The lawyer continued, "there are two conditions for you to receive this offer. One, you must always use the name of Pip. Second, the name of your guardian③ and provider is to remain a secret, until that person chooses to tell you. You must not try to discover who the person is, or ask any questions to

① **(not) stand in sb.'s way**（不）阻止某人做某事
② **speak for oneself** 发表个人意见；表达自己的意思
③ **guardian** /ˈɡɑːdɪən/ *n.* 法定监护人

find out. Do you accept these conditions?"

I could hardly whisper, "Yes."

"Now, as for details. You will move to London for your study. You have been given enough money to live the life of a gentleman while there. I will provide you with all your needs while you live there. I have also suggested that you use Mr. Matthew Pocket as a teacher." When I heard the name "Matthew", I remembered the name of one of Miss Havisham's relations who did not visit her often. "You must buy some new clothes," he continued. "Shall I leave you twenty pounds?" He took this out of his large purse and placed the coins onto the table. "When is it possible for you to come to London? Next Saturday?"

Still feeling very confused, I agreed. Looking at Joe, I saw he was even more confused.

"Well, Joe Gargery? It's not my decision to promise you anything," he said, throwing his purse from one hand to another, "but perhaps I have been told to give you a present when you lose your worker and student."

Joe rested his great strong hand on my shoulder

in the gentlest possible way. "Pip is free to go after[①] his fortune and happiness, he knows that. Money can never pay me back for losing the little child— who came to the iron workshop—or the best of my friends!" He could not continue.

Dear good Joe! How ungrateful I was, so ready to leave you! I can still see the tears on your cheeks when you said those words. At the time I was too excited by my good luck to remember what I owed to Joe[②]. Mr. Jaggers clearly thought Joe was making a mistake in refusing money. He looked oddly[③] at Joe and then left the house, telling me to be at his office in London in a week's time.

Joe told Biddy about our meeting with Mr. Jaggers, and she congratulated me. Both she and Joe were very quiet and sad at first, but I promised I would not forget them or the iron workshop and would often return home to visit them. Biddy tried to explain what had happened to my sister, but the poor woman could not understand.

Joe and Biddy became more cheerful talking

---

① **go after...** 设法得到……
② **owe sth. to sb.** 欠某人某物
③ **oddly** /ˈɒdlɪ/ *adv.* 奇怪地

about my future, but I began to feel quite different. Now that I was going to be a gentleman, as I had always wished, I felt miserable. I didn't know if I wanted to leave my home, my former life of happy memories.

That week passed slowly. I took a last walk through the churchyard to the wetlands to see my parents' grave. I felt relieved that I needed never think about my prisoner again. I was quite sure he was dead by now.

I decided to ask something special of Biddy. "Biddy," I said, "do you think you could teach Joe a bit?"

"Teach him?" asked Biddy.

"Well, I thought since you're so good at teaching me, maybe you can do the same for Joe. I love him more than anyone else, but his education and manners could be better."

Biddy opened her eyes very wide. "Oh?!" she said. "So his manners aren't good enough, then?"

"Oh, there's no need to improve them for here, but after I receive my fortune, he'll need to meet important people, and behave correctly. He'll need an education in manners."

"Maybe," said Biddy, looking away from me, "he wouldn't want to meet all those important people of yours. Maybe he wouldn't want to leave his job that he does so well or the village where he's loved?"

"Biddy," I said, angry at her reply, "are you jealous① of my good luck? I certainly didn't expect this of you."

"Just remember that I'll always do my best for the family. And I'll always remember you, whatever you think of me," said poor Biddy.

This interview did not please me, and I noted it strange that the news of my expectations had made me a little unhappier.

Mr. Pumblechook was waiting for me at the door of his shop when I went into town to order my new clothes.

"My dear friend, that is, if you allow me to call you that," he cried, grabbing both my hands and shaking them. "Let me congratulate you on your great fortune! Nobody deserves it more than you!" After ordering the clothes, I agreed to join him for

---

① **jealous** /ˈdʒeləs/ *adj.* 嫉妒的

lunch.

"When I think," he said happily, "that I, by taking you to play, might have had a small part^① in helping you with Miss—"

I stopped him before he could continue. "Remember that we must never say anything about the person who is being so generous to me."

"Don't worry, my dear friend, you can trust me! Have some wine, have some chicken! Oh chicken," he said, addressing the meal, "I'm sure you never thought when you were running around on the farm you would be lucky enough to be lunch for one who—May I? May I?" and he stood up to shake my hand again.

Pumblechook reminded me of all the happy times he and I had spent together during my childhood. I did not remember those times as happy, at least on my part, but I began to feel Pumblechook was a good-hearted, sincere man. Later, he asked my advice on a business matter. He was looking to find a young gentleman to put money into his business, and he seemed very interested in

---

① **part (in sth.)**（活动中的）个人部分；作用；本分

my opinion. "And may I? May I?" He stood up to shake hands with me again.

"You know, I always thought to myself, 'One day that boy will make his fortune①. He's no ordinary boy.'" I thought he had certainly kept his opinion very secret while I was growing up.

There was one person I had to visit before going to London. I was dressed in my new clothes and went to Miss Havisham's house. Her cousin opened the gate for me again.

"Well, Pip?" Miss Havisham said when she saw me.

"Tomorrow I'll leave for London, Miss Havisham," I said, choosing my words carefully. "I've come to say goodbye. I've had much luck since I saw you last, and I'm so grateful for it!"

"Good, good!" she replied. She looked delightedly at her cousin, who was staring at my new clothes. "I've heard of your good fortune from Mr. Jaggers. It seems a rich person has decided to provide for you?"

"Yes, Miss Havisham."

---

① **fortune** /ˈfɔːtʃən/ *n.* 命运；运气；财富

She smiled cruelly at her cousin, who was looking rather ill and uncomfortable.

"Remember, do whatever Mr. Jaggers tells you. I know you are to always keep the name of Pip. You will do this, won't you? Goodbye, Pip." She gave me her hand and I kissed it. Then I left the old lady in her yellow bride's dress sitting in the dark candle light, surrounded by dusty furniture.

Being in such a hurry on Saturday morning, I only said a quick goodbye to my family, and set out to walk the few miles into town to catch the coach to London. The mist over the wetlands was rising as I left the peaceful sleeping village, as if showing me the great unknown world I was entering. I suddenly realized all I was leaving behind—my childhood, my home, and Joe. I wished I had asked Joe to accompany[1] me to the coach, and I could not stop crying. Throughout the journey, whenever the horses were changed, I thought with an aching heart about getting down and going back to say a proper goodbye. But the mist had already disappeared, and my new world lay ahead of me.

---

① **accompany** /əˈkʌmpənɪ/ *vt.* 陪同

Chapter 7
Arriving in London

I had heard from everybody in England that London was a wonderful city. So I was quite surprised to find narrow dirty streets with people crowded into tiny houses. I thought it rather ugly. The size of London frightened me. Going to Smithfield, the meat market, shocked me—there was dirt and blood everywhere. Then I walked past Newgate Prison where prisoners were hanged. A drunken man excitedly told me that four men would die there tomorrow. This news disgusted me. I don't think my first impression of London could have been any worse.

I finally managed to find Mr. Jaggers' office, where several other people were waiting for him too. After some time he appeared and walked towards me. When his clients saw him, they all rushed together at him. Some he spoke to and others he pushed away. One man held on to his sleeve[①].

---

① **sleeve** /sli:v/ *n.* 袖子

"Please, Mr. Jaggers," he cried, "the police say my brother has stolen some silver. You are the only person who can save him! I'm ready to pay anything!"

"Your brother?" repeated the lawyer. "The trial is tomorrow? Well, I'm sorry for both you and him, but I'm the side of the court."

"No, Mr. Jaggers!" begged the man with tears in his eyes. "I'll pay anything! Don't say you're against him!"

"Out of my way," said Mr. Jaggers. We left the man begging on his knees①.

Mr. Jaggers then turned to me and said that on Monday I would be going to Matthew Pocket's house to begin my studies, but until then I would be staying with his son, Herbert. Herbert lived nearby.

Mr. Jaggers' clerk, Wemmick, led me to Mr. Pocket's rooms. Wemmick was a short man with a square face that gave no expressions. He was between forty and fifty years old. His mouth was so wide it reminded of a post-box, and this made him look like he was smiling all the time.

---

① **knee** /niː/ *n.* 膝盖

As we walked, I tried to make conversation with him. "Is London a very wicked place?" I asked.

"People are robbed or murdered in London, but that can happen to people anywhere, if the criminal can profit by it."

With people like Wemmick accepting crime so calmly, I was not sure about living in London.

The building that Herbert Pocket lived in was the dirtiest I had ever seen, with broken windows and dusty doors. In the middle was a little square with dying trees all around. I gave a look of horror at Mr. Wemmick.

Not understanding my look, he replied, "You must be pleased. Its quietness must make you think of the country. I do agree. Goodbye, Mr. Pip."

I went up the stairs and found a note on Mr. Pocket's door, saying "Returning soon." I heard footsteps about half an hour later, and a young man, quite out of breath① and of my age, appeared at the door. "Mr. Pip?" he said. "I'm very sorry I'm so late!"

I was unable to believe my eyes, and looked at

---

① **(be) out of/short of breath** 呼吸急促；上气不接下气。 hold one's breath 暂时屏住呼吸

him in confusion. Suddenly he looked closely at me and started in surprise.

"You're the boy I fought with at Miss Havisham's!"

"And you," I said, "are the pale young gentleman!"

We shook hands and had a good laugh together.

"Well!" he said, "I hope you'll be kind enough to forgive me for knocking you down that day." Actually, I had knocked him down but I did not tell him so.

"I had been invited to Miss Havisham's to see if she liked me," he began. "I suppose she didn't have a good impression of me. Otherwise, I could be a rich man now and may be even engaged① to Estella."

"Were you disappointed?" I asked.

"That I'm not engaged to Estella? Oh no! I wouldn't want to marry her! Miss Havisham raised her to be proud and hard so that she can break men's hearts, as a revenge on all men."

"Is she related to Miss Havisham?" I asked.

"No, only adopted. So tell me why you were at Miss Havisham's."

---

① **engage** /ɪnˈɡeɪdʒ/ *vt.* 使……订婚。只用于 be/get/become engaged to sb. 结构。

"The same as you—to make my fortune! But I was lucky."

"Mr. Jaggers is Miss Havisham's lawyer. I'm very glad that he suggested my father to teach you. My father is Miss Havisham's cousin, you know."

I could tell that Herbert Pocket was an open and honest man, and he made an excellent impression on me. His character had nothing secret or mean and we soon became close friends. I told him of my former life in the village, and my future expectations.

"Call me Herbert," he said. "Would you mind if I called you by the nickname Handel? Handel wrote a wonderful piece of music called The Ironworker and it reminds me of you." I agreed of course, and during dinner, Herbert told me Miss Havisham's sad story.

"Her mother was married to a very rich and proud man, but she died at a young age. Miss Havisham was their only child. Then the father married his cook, and they had a son together. This son, Miss Havisham's half-brother①, was not a good

---
① **half-brother** 同父异母或同母异父的兄弟

person, and his father did not leave him as much money as he left Miss Havisham. Her half-brother wanted revenge because he thought that she had influenced her father against him."

"Anyway, a certain man came and pretended to be in love with Miss Havisham. It's true she was certainly in love with him, for she gave him whatever money he asked for. My father was the only one of her relatives to tell her that she should not trust this man. This made her so angry that she told my father to leave the house immediately, and to this day he has never seen her again. Because her other relations were only interested in getting some of her wealth, they said nothing. The wedding day was fixed, guests were invited, and her dress and the cake were brought to the house. The day arrived, but the man did not. Instead, he wrote a letter—"

"Did she receive this letter at twenty to nine, when she was dressing for her wedding?" I said.

"Yes, and since then her clocks have been stopped and her windows not opened. She was very ill for a while. Nobody knows what happened to the man, but people think that her half-brother sent him to get money from her, and that he shared the profits. Perhaps he hated her for taking most of the Havisham fortune. So now you know as much as I do!"

We moved onto other things. I asked Herbert about his profession.

"Oh, I work in the city," he said happily. "Insuring[1] ships. A lot of money in that, you know. Very big profits!"

I began to think that Herbert's expectations must be greater than mine.

"And where are your ships at now?" I asked.

"Oh, I'm still working in a counting house just now. I don't get paid very much, but I'm looking for a good opportunity. Then I'll begin on my ships and make my fortune!"

I could see from the old, worn furniture[2] in the room that Herbert must be very poor. I thought that although he was full of hopes for the future, he would never be very rich or successful.

We spent a happy weekend together visiting

---

① **insure** /ɪnˈʃʊə/ vt. 保险；投保。insure sb./sth. (against sth.) 为……保险

② **furniture** /ˈfɜːnɪtʃə/ n. (总称) 家具，为不可数名词

London. It was all very new and exciting, but I could not help noticing the dirt and bad smells and heat. When I thought of my village home, I became quite sad. My home seemed so far away.

Chapter 8
A Visit to Mr. Wemmick and Mr. Jaggers

Herbert introduced me to his father, who lived on the other side of London, in Hammersmith. I studied hard with Mr. Pocket for a few months, and I found him always a most① kind and helpful teacher. I spent half my time at Herbert's and half at his father's home. When I needed money, I went to collect it from Wemmick at Mr. Jaggers' office. There was always plenty of money available.

Two other gentlemen were also studying at Mr. Pocket's. One of them, Bentley Drummle, came from a wealthy family that lived in the country. He was lazy, proud, mean and stupid. I was friendlier with Startop, a pleasant, caring young man. We used to row our boats together up and down the river. But Herbert remained my greatest friend, and we spent most of our time together.

One day Wemmick invited me to his house at

---
① **a most** 极；很；非常

Walworth, which is a village outside of London.

"Do you mind walking there, Mr. Pip?" he asked. "I like to get exercise when I can. Tonight for dinner we're going to have a roast chicken. It was a little present from one of my clients, and I think it'll be especially good. I like receiving gifts from clients, especially if it's cash, or something that can be changed easily into cash. These rings I'm wearing were given to me by clients, just before they died. All of them were hanged, they were. By the way, I hope you won't mind meeting my aged^① parent, would you?"

"No, of course not," I replied.

"Have you had dinner with Mr. Jaggers yet?" Wemmick continued. "I know tomorrow he'll invite you and the other three young gentlemen. There's always good food and drink at his house. But I'll tell you that when you're there, take a good look at his housekeeper."

"Why?" I asked. "What's so special about his housekeeper?"

"She's like a wild animal that Mr. Jaggers has

---

① **aged** /ˈeɪdʒd/ *adj.* 作定语，表示 "极老的，年老的"

trained! Oh yes! He's the strongest and cleverest man in London. Another strange thing about him, you know, is that he never locks his doors or windows at night."

"And he's never been robbed?" I asked, surprised.

"None of the thieves in London would dare rob him, even though they know where he lives. They are all afraid of him, you see. He wouldn't rest until he had hanged every single one. He's a powerful man, Mr. Pip."

Mr. Wemmick led me to a tiny wooden house in the middle of a garden. On top of the house's roof was a small gun.

"At nine o'clock every evening we fire the gun," Wemmick said proudly. "And behind the house, which I call the Castle, I raise animals and even grow my own vegetables. So, in case an enemy attacks us, we can always eat our own food. What do you think of it?"

I told him his home was wonderful and congratulated him on his ideas①. Clearly he was delighted to show visitors his ideas and improvements.

---

① **congratulate sb. on sth.** 祝贺某人……

"Everything I did myself, you know," he said, "When I do things around the house, it helps me forget the office for a while. Would it be all right if I were to introduce you to the Aged now? He would like it very much."

We entered the Castle and found a cheerful old man sitting by the fire.

"Well, aged parent," said Wemmick, "how are you doing?"

"Quite well, John," replied the old man, happily.

"This here is Mr. Pip, Aged Parent. Mr. Pip, he's completely deaf and can't understand a word you say, but he likes to nod at people and see people nod back at him."

"This is my son's fine house, sir," cried the old man, nodding back at me. "I think the nation should keep it for public visit after my son's death."

"Proud of it, aren't you, Aged?" said Wemmick. I noticed that his face had lost its usual hardness when he looked at the old man.

"Does Mr. Jaggers admire your home, Mr. Wemmick?" I asked.

"He's never been here as I've never invited

him. Never met the Aged, either. No, the office is one thing and my private life is another. I never speak of the Castle at the office, and don't think of the office at the Castle."

The Aged told me that he was looking forward to the evening firing of the gun. Exactly at nine o'clock, Wemmick fired it. The tiny house shook, and the Aged excitedly jumped up and down in his armchair①, crying, "I heard it! I heard the gun!"

After an excellent supper, I spent the night in the smallest bedroom I had ever been in. The next morning, while walking back to London with Wemmick, I noticed that his face was becoming dryer and harder, and his mouth more like a post-box again. At the office, it seemed impossible to guess that he had a home, or an aged parent, or any interests outside of his work.

Wemmick was correct in saying that Mr. Jaggers would invite me to dinner. Startop, Drummle, Herbert and I went to the office at six o'clock the next evening. We found Jaggers washing his hands and face carefully with his perfumed soap. This was what he

---

① **armchair** /ɑːmˈtʃeə(r)/ *n.* 扶手椅；单人沙发

85

did every evening before returning home. It was as if he washed away his clients and his work, like dirt. Then we all walked to his house together.

When the housekeeper brought in the first dish, I took a good look at her. She was about forty and had a strange wild expression on her pale face. Toward her master she seemed almost afraid, and would look anxiously at him whenever she entered the room.

The food was very good indeed, and the conversation was cheerful. But Mr. Jaggers somehow made us show the worst side of our characters. He encouraged Drummle, who we all thought a little bothersome①, to further annoy② us. Drummle proudly said that he was stronger than any of us, and we all foolishly showed each other our muscles, trying to prove how strong we were. Suddenly Mr. Jaggers loudly clapped his large hand on the housekeeper's, just as she was removing a dish from the table. This stopped us talking immediately.

"Gentlemen," he said, "My housekeeper here is stronger than any of you. Show them your wrists,

---

① **bothersome** /ˈbɒðəsəm/ *adj.* 引起麻烦的；困扰人的

② **annoy** /əˈnɔɪ/ *vt.* 使烦恼（生气）；打扰

Molly."

"No, please, master," she begged. She tried to pull away, but he held her firmly by the hand.

"Go on, Molly," he ordered, and she held her wrists out to us. "You'll never see stronger hands than these," he said. We all thought his display rather strange, and there was uncomfortable silence for a few minutes. Then Mr. Jaggers said, "All right, Molly, you can go," and she hurried out. He did not give us an explanation.

Mr. Jaggers continued to enjoy watching us quarrelling with Drummle during the rest of our dinner. He seemed, surprisingly, to like Drummle very much. I was glad when the dinner was over, and Herbert and I walked quietly back to our rooms together.

Chapter 9
Joe Comes to Visit

*M*y dear Pip,

    Mr. Gargery asks me to let you know that he will be in London soon. He asks to visit you at 9 o'clock on Tuesday morning at Mr. Herbert Pocket's rooms, if it is all right with you. We talk about you every night, and wonder what your life is like in London.

Best wishes,

Biddy

P.S.[①] *Please do not refuse to see him, even though you are a gentleman now. Joe is such a good man.*

Because I received this letter on Monday, I realized that Joe would arrive the next morning. I did not look forward to seeing him at all. In fact if money could have kept him away, I certainly would have paid money.

His clothes, his manners and uneducated way of speaking would make me ashamed[②]. I knew that

---
① **P.S.** = postscript 来信的附言
② **ashamed** /əˈʃeɪmd/ *adj.* 羞耻（惭愧）的

luckily Herbert would not laugh at him.

I heard Joe's loud boots on the stairs at nine o'clock the next morning. At last he entered Herbert's rooms.

"I'm very glad to see you, Joe. Give me your hat."

But he insisted that he hold it carefully in front of him. He was wearing his best suit, which he looked quite uncomfortable in.

"Well! You've become quite a gentleman, Pip!"

"And you are looking wonderfully well, Joe."

"Yes, thank God. Your poor sister is no worse though no better. And Biddy is still as hard working. But Wopsle has become an actor, acting in one of your London theatres, he is!" Joe's eyes looked around the room. Recently I had bought a lot of expensive furniture, and he did not miss① noticing these things.

"Join us for breakfast, please, Mr. Gargery," said Herbert politely. Joe looked round for a place to put his hat, and finally settled on laying it on a shelf. I did not enjoy breakfast. It was a painful experience for me. Joe would wave his fork in the

---

① **miss** /mɪs/ *vt.* 未见到；未击中；未达到（目标）

air so much that he dropped more than he ate, and I was glad when Herbert left to go to work. I wasn't caring enough to realize that it was my fault that he acted this way, because I considered him common.

"As we are now alone, sir—" began Joe.

"Joe," I said angrily, "call me Pip, not sir!"

He was quiet for a moment. "I wouldn't have come, you see," he began slowly and carefully. "I wouldn't have breakfast with you gentlemen, if I didn't have to. I've a message for you, Pip. Miss Havisham asked me to come and tell you that Estella's returned home and would be glad to see you."

The blood rushed to my face as soon as I heard her name.

"Now that[①] I've given my message to you," said Joe, "I'll leave." He stood and picked up his hat. "Pip, I wish you even more success."

"Are you leaving so soon, Joe?" I asked.

"Yes." he said firmly. Our eyes met, and all the "sirs" melted out of his honest heart as we shook hands. "Pip, my dear boy, life is full of so many goodbyes. I'm an ironworker, and you're a

---

① **now (that)...** 由于，既然，that 可省。

gentleman. Apart is how we live. It's not that I'm proud, but I want to be where I feel right. You can see these clothes are all wrong for me. And I'm wrong in London. But I'm fine at the iron workshop, or in the kitchen, or on the wetlands. Joe, the ironworker, at the old iron workshop, doing the old work—there's nothing wrong in that. You'll see I'm right when you come down to see us. I know I'm slow and stupid, but I've understood this. And so God bless you, Pip, dear old boy, God bless you!"

His words were spoken simply and from the heart. They touched me deeply, but by the time I was able to control my tears, he had already gone.

I decided I would visit Miss Havisham as soon as possible. When I arrived to take my seat on the coach to our town the next day, I realized I was sitting in front of two prisoners. They were being taken to the prison-ships near our village. The prisoners wore handcuffs, and iron chains on their legs. Suddenly I recognized one of them and was frozen[①] with horror—it was the same man in our village pub who had given me the two pound notes!

---

① **freeze** /friːz/ *vt.* 本意为 "结冰，凝固"，此处指 "（因恐惧、震惊等）使不能活动"。

Strangely enough, the prisoners were talking about it during our journey.

"So Magwitch asked you to give the boy two pounds?"

"I did what he asked. You see, the boy had helped him. Gave him food and kept his secret."

"What ever happened to Magwitch?"

"He was sent to Australia for life after he tried to escape from the prison-ship."

Having grown into a young man I was not worried that the prisoner would recognize me, but I was afraid all the same①. The horror of my childhood experience with the escaped prisoner quickly came back to me, as if not letting me forget it.

But as soon as we arrived and I was going to Miss Havisham's house, I thought only of my future and bright hopes. She had adopted Estella; she had also more or less adopted me. Perhaps she wanted me to live in the dark old house and marry Estella. Still, I knew I would be unhappy with Estella, even though I loved her. I loved her because I couldn't

---

① **all the same** 仍然；还是；反正

stop myself loving her.

I was both shocked and surprised to see Orlick opening the gate for me.

"You aren't working for Joe any more?" I asked.

"As you see, no, young master," he said rudely.

I decided I would tell Mr. Jaggers that Orlick was not to be trusted and shouldn't work for Miss Havisham. I hoped Mr. Jaggers would then send him away.

There was a well-dressed lady sitting with Miss Havisham when I entered her room. When she lifted her head and looked at me, I knew it was Estella. How beautiful she had become! But I felt very far from her. I still felt like the rough, common boy she used to laugh at.

Laughing wickedly, Miss Havisham said, "She's changed very much, hasn't she, Pip?" I didn't know how to reply. Estella was still very proud. I knew she was the reason why I felt ashamed of home, and of Joe. But I also knew that I could never stop loving her.

We walked together in the old garden and talked quietly about our childhood times. Now that we were older, it seemed easier for her to accept me as a friend. I could not have been happier. I was quite sure that Miss Havisham had planned for us to be together. What a fool I was!

She suddenly stopped and turned to me. "Miss Havisham will want us to spend more time together in the future. But I must warn you I have no heart①. Don't expect me to fall in love."

"I don't think that's true," I replied. She looked straight at me and I recognized something in her face. It reminded me of an expression I had seen recently, on another woman.

When we went back inside the house, Miss Havisham asked to speak to me alone. "Do you still admire her, Pip?" she asked eagerly.

"Everybody who sees her must do so."

She pulled my head closer to hers with her bony arm and whispered in my ear, "Love her, love her, love her! If she likes you, love her! If she hurts you, love her! If she tears your heart to pieces, love her!" She seemed so angry I thought she was talking about hate, or revenge, or death, not love.

① **have no heart** 没有心情。heart 本意为 "心脏"，在此指 "热心，热情"，不可数名词。

95

Chapter 10
Pip and Herbert Discuss Love

I returned to London, dreaming of Estella, now a beautiful woman who I hoped would share my future life. I needed to speak to someone about my feelings. That evening I told Herbert my secret.

My friend wasn't surprised. Instead, he replied:

"I already know that, Handel. It was obvious, even though you never told me. You've always loved Estella. I think it's very lucky that you have a chance to marry her. Does she—ah—admire① you?"

I sadly shook my head. "No, she doesn't. You may think me lucky, Herbert. I have great expectations, I know. But they are nothing without her! Also, I still don't really know how much money I'll receive, or when! Nothing is certain!"

"Now, Handel," said Herbert cheerfully, "don't give up hope. Mr. Jaggers himself said you would have quite a large fortune, didn't he? He's always

① **admire** /əd'maɪə/ vt. 钦佩，赞美；（口语）想要；喜欢。admire to do sth. 很想做某事，此处取"喜欢"意。

96

right about money, isn't he? Anyway, you'll soon be twenty-one. Perhaps you'll know more after your birthday."

"Thank you, Herbert!" I said, feeling much better.

"But I want you to think about Estella, my dear Handel," said Herbert, looking serious. "Her education is very high, and you may be unhappy with her. Isn't it possibly, and I'm saying this as a friend, is it possible to forget about her?"

"I know you're right," I said, feeling quite miserable, "but I can never stop loving her."

"Well, no matter!" said Herbert. "I have something to tell you myself. I am engaged."

"What's the young lady's name?"

"Her name is Clara. Her mother died recently and she lives with her father. We love each other but we have to keep our feelings secret for now. I haven't enough money to marry her yet. Once I start insuring ships we can get married." Herbert tried to manage his usual cheerful smile, but he didn't seem hopeful about the future.

One day I received a letter from Estella, and

my heart beat fast.

"I will be in London the day after tomorrow on the midday coach. Miss Havisham wants you to meet me. Estella."

I would have ordered several new suits if there had been enough time. I waited all morning impatiently for her coach. When I saw her, she seemed more beautiful than ever, and her manner to me was very pleasant. I took her to the house in London that Miss Havisham had arranged for her stay. It seemed that Miss Havisham had her life planned① right down to the smallest detail. I could only hope that I was also part of that plan.

---

① **have her life planned** 是 have sth. done 结构，让某事被他人做。

Chapter 11
Pip Goes to a Funeral

A black-edged envelope was delivered to me at Herbert's rooms one evening. It informed[1] me that Mrs. J. Gargery had died the previous Monday, and that the burial would be next Monday, at 3 p.m. I was shocked by this news. I had never had someone close to me die before, and even though I had never loved my sister, I could not imagine life without her.

It was early Monday afternoon when I arrived at the iron workshop. Joe was sitting in the front room, dressed in a black cloak.

"Dear Joe, how are you?" I asked.

"Pip, my dear boy, she was a fine woman when you knew her..." and he could say no more.

Biddy was dressed in a neat little black dress and was busy serving food. There were old friends from the village in the front room, talking quietly among themselves. I noticed old fool Pumblechook looking at me

---

① **inform** /ɪnˈfɔːm/ *vt.* 告诉，通知；告发（密）

as he drank wine and swallowed large pieces of cake.

"May I, my dear sir? May I?" he asked with his mouth full, and shook my hand with great feeling.

They carried my sister's dead body slowly out of the house and through the village. We followed behind. Beyond the wetlands we could see the sails of ships on the river. There, in the churchyard, next to my unknown parents, my poor sister was laid to rest in the earth, while birds sang and clouds danced in the sky.

Biddy, Joe and I felt much better when all the guests had gone. We had a quiet supper together. I decided to spend the night with them at the iron workshop, and this pleased Joe very much. I was also quite pleased with myself for offering to do so.

Later I found Biddy alone and said, "I guess you won't be able to stay here now, will you, Biddy?"

"No, Mr. Pip. I'll be staying in the village. I'll still look after Mr. Gargery as much as I can."

"But how are you going to live, Biddy? If you need any money—"

My offer had made her cheeks turn red, "I'm going to be the village schoolteacher," she said

quickly. "I can earn① my own money."

"How did my sister die, Biddy?"

"She had been more ill than usual recently. One evening she said 'Joe' very clearly. I ran to the iron workshop to fetch him. She put her arms around his neck and laid her head on his shoulder, quite happy. Then she said 'Sorry', and after that 'Pip'. She didn't lift her head up again, and one hour later she died."

Biddy cried, and I cried too.

"What about Orlick, Biddy?"

"He still lives in the village, but he doesn't work for Miss Havisham any more. Sometimes, you know, he—he follows me."

"I want you to tell me if he bothers you, Biddy. I'll be coming here more often now. I don't want to leave poor Joe alone."

Biddy said nothing.

"Come, Biddy, why are you silent?"

"Are you sure you will come to see him?"

"Oh Biddy!" I said sadly. "What a bad side to your character! Don't say anything more!" All through that evening I thought how unkind and

---

① **earn** /ɜːn/ *vt.* 赚（挣；获得）

unjust Biddy was to me.

The next morning I found Joe already hard at work in the iron workshop. I said goodbye to him before leaving.

"I return to see you soon, Joe! Don't worry!"

"It'll never be too soon, sir," said Joe, "and never too often, Pip!"

As I walked away to the village, I knew that I would not go back. Biddy was right.

Back in London, I did some serious thinking about my character. I could see that it had not improved any since hearing about my expectations. I also knew I was spending far too much money. What was worse, this was a bad influence on Herbert, as he began spending too much as well. He had many bills, and I offered to pay for them, but he was too proud to accept my offer. On my twenty-first birthday I had hoped to discover more about my future, but Mr. Jaggers would not give me any more information, explaining that he wasn't allowed to. He did tell me that I was now to have five hundred pounds a year to spend as I liked. Then I suddenly thought of a way to help Herbert.

I asked Wemmick to advise me on helping a friend start up in① business, and his post-box mouth opened wide.

"Go to one of the six London bridges," he said, "and throw all your money over it. That's a better way than investing money in a friend. Of course, that's my professional opinion."

"But if I was a customer at Walworth, you would give me a different opinion?"

"You're most welcome there, Mr. Pip, on private business."

The next Sunday I went to visit Wemmick and his aged parent at the Castle. There was a lady called Miss Skiffins this time. She was clearly a regular visitor, and she made the tea and sat next to Wemmick on the sofa. When Wemmick and I were alone, he listened carefully to my request, and after thinking hard for a while, he came up with an answer.

I arranged to invest some money with his help in② a shipping company called Clarrikers. I signed an agreement with them where they promised to offer Herbert a job. Later, they would

① **start (sb.) up in...**（使某人）开始从事……
② **invest money in...** 在……投资

agree to make him a partner. I finally felt that my expectations had brought good to someone other than[①] myself.

---

① **other than** *prep.* 除了（所说的不包括在内）

Chapter 12
Pip and the Truth

I often visited Estella while she lived in London with friends of Miss Havisham's. She had a large number of admirers, and I became jealous of all of them. I still thought about her, day and night, and my dearest wish was to marry her, even though I was never happy with her. Miss Havisham ordered me several times to bring Estella to visit her, and I always obeyed, of course. Estella was still as proud and cold as ever, and she was this way with her admirers, with Miss Havisham and with me.

One admirer of hers was unpleasant Bentley Drummle. One day I asked her about him.

"Estella, why do you keep encouraging someone like Drummle? Nobody likes him, and he's stupid."

"Don't be a fool, Pip. You're so much like a child," she answered. "I encourage him because it has a certain effect on① my other admirers."

---

① **have an effect on...** 对……有影响（作用）

"He isn't worth your encouragement!" I cried angrily.

"If I smile at him, it's because it means nothing to me. At least I am always honest with you and don't give you false looks or smiles. You should be glad."

My heart was aching for Estella, but I had no idea that a horrible event would happen that would completely destroy my hopes and dreams. Events which had begun before I ever met her were slowly reaching their end.

Herbert and I had moved to live in rooms in a house by the river, in the Temple area of London. He was abroad on business① one evening when I was alone at home, reading. The weather was terrible, stormy and wet, and the streets were covered with deep mud. The wind off of the river shook the whole building. As I finished reading and closed my book at eleven o'clock, I heard a heavy footstep on the stairs. I went to the door with my lamp and saw a man coming slowly upstairs. He was about sixty and was wearing rough clothes. He had a brown face and long gray hair. What both surprised

① **on business** 因公（事）；出差

and frightened me was that he was holding out both hands to me.

I was polite but cold. "Can I help you?" I asked.

"Ah! Yes," he said and dropped his hands. "Yes, I'll explain." He entered into the sitting room and looked admiringly at my furniture and books. Then he held out his hands to me again, but I would not take them. He sat down in a chair①, rubbed his eyes with one rather dirty hand, and looked at me.

"Ah," he said, "it's disappointing, it is. I've looked forward to this day for so long, I have. Still it's not your fault. Is there anybody near who can hear us?"

"Why are you, a stranger, asking me that question?" I asked. Then I knew who he was! In spite of all the years that had passed, I knew for certain that he was my prisoner! When he held out his hands again, I took them. He raised my hands to his lips and kissed them.

"I've never forgotten how you helped me all those years ago, Pip!" He tried to put his arms around me, but I stopped him.

"If you are still grateful for what I did in my

---

① **in a chair** 与 on a chair 有区别。用 in 表示坐在有扶手的椅子上；用 on 表示坐在没有扶手的椅子上。

childhood, then I hope you have changed your bad ways and improved your way of life now. Why have you come here to thank me? It wasn't necessary. You must understand that..." I stopped speaking when I noticed how he was staring at me with his mouth open.

"What is it I understand?" he asked, his eyes fixed on me.

"That you and I met once in the past, but I don't wish to be your friend. Our lives are separate. Do you want to have a drink before you leave?" I noticed that his eyes were full of tears. "I'm sorry if I sound too hard." I added. "I didn't mean to be. Let's hope for good luck in your future!" We drank together. "Where have you been living recently?"

"I escaped from the prison-ship, as you know, so I was sent to Australia. After several years I finished my punishment, and so I was allowed to work for myself. I did every kind of job there. I made a lot of money, but it was a hard life."

"I'm glad to hear that you were successful," I said. "That reminds me—I have the two pounds you sent me long ago. Thank you but I don't need it now." I handed him two new pound notes from my purse. Then he held the notes over the lamp until they caught fire①.

"May I ask," he said, "how it is you've done so well since I met you on those lonely wetlands?" I began to shake, and he fixed his eyes on mine.

"I—I've been chosen to receive a fortune so that I may become a gentleman," I whispered.

"I'd like to guess how much," said the prisoner. "Could it be, perhaps, five hundred pounds a year?" I stood up quickly, holding on to the back of my chair with my heart beating like a hammer. I felt my entire world move.

"Is your agent," he continued, "is he perhaps a lawyer by the name of② Jaggers?"

Suddenly, I knew the awful truth about my fortune. I could neither speak nor breathe, and I fell on to the sofa. Bringing his worn, old face close to mine, he bent over me.

"Yes, Pip, dear boy, you've guessed the truth that I'm the person who made a gentleman of you!

---

① **fire** /ˈfaɪə/ *n.* 火。注意与"火"搭配的短语: 1) set fire to 点燃; 2) catch fire 着火; 3) on fire 烧着; 4) fight the fire 救火

② **by the name of** 称(叫)作

You see, while I was in Australia I promised myself that all the money I earned should go to you—I'm your second father, Pip! I didn't go to school and I'm not a gentleman myself, but I've got you, Pip! Just look what a gentleman you are, and the education and books you have! One day you'll read them to me, Pip, even if I can't understand them! Didn't you ever think that I could be the person sending you the money?"

"Oh no, no, no," I replied. "Never, never! Wasn't anyone else involved?"

"No, just me, and Jaggers. Dear boy, I want you to understand that I kept myself going just by thinking of you. I promised myself I'd come back to England one day and see you grown into a gentleman." He laid his hand on my shoulder. "Find a bed for me to sleep in," he said. "And this is most important—not a word to anybody! I'll be hanged if they know I've come back. Remember I was sent away for life."

I was horribly confused. A man whom I could not like, who had paid for my education and luxuries for years, had come to see me, even though it meant he was putting his life in danger. My whole body shook with disgust when he touched me, but I also had to protect him.

He slept in Herbert's room. I carefully locked all the doors and then sat weakly down by the fire, trying to make sense of① my life. How foolish my dreams now seemed! Miss Havisham had never wanted to make me rich. And she had no plans to let me marry Estella. But what was worse was that this prisoner, who could be caught and hanged at any moment, was the reason I had left my life with Joe and Biddy. I knew I could never, never, never forgive myself for that.

---

① **make sense of** 弄懂……的意思

Chapter 13
Magwitch's Future and Past

I woke early, even though I had only slept a little. I wanted some fresh air, so I walked downstairs and out of the building. On the way down the stairs I fell over a man hiding in a dark corner. He ran away immediately, which worried me. I thought that maybe he had followed my prisoner to the house. Was he now going to tell police?

My guest and I ate breakfast together. I tried hard not to be disgusted by his manners, but he ate noisily and greedily, like an animal. He told me his name was Abel Magwitch. After breakfast, he lit his pipe and held out his hands to me again.

"Let me have a look at you, dear boy!" he said. "A real gentleman you are, made by me! You'll have everything a London gentleman should—a carriage, horses, everything!" He threw a large thick wallet onto the table. "All that money is yours. Let me see you spend it."

"Stop!" I cried. "We must talk about your

plans. How long are you planning to stay here?"

"How long?" he repeated, surprised. "I'm not going back to Australia, if that's what you mean."

"But you're not safe here."

"Dear boy, who knows I'm here? You, Jaggers and Wemmick, that's all. Anyway, I've lived with the fear of death all my life."

I knew I had to keep him out of sight at least until Herbert returned. Together I thought we could produce a better plan for the future. I rented a room for him in a house that was near ours. I thought he would be safer there. Then I bought him different clothes and took him for a haircut. But he looked just the same to me, and I was in constant fear that someone who had known him in the past would recognize him.

We spent five long days and evenings together, and the weather was particularly bad. The wind and rain beat on the windows, and made those few days seem like a year to me. My unwanted① guest didn't do much. He slept, or ate, or played cards. Sometimes he would listen to me read, and then

① **unwanted** /ˈʌnˈwɒntɪd/ *adj.* 不受欢迎的

smile proudly. Not being able to sleep or eat, I was in quite bad shape①. I used to watch him sleep, wondering what sort of bloody crimes were in his past, and knowing that I alone had to protect him from a horrible death.

When Herbert finally returned, I was relieved. At last I could share my terrible news with my friend. He, too, was greatly shocked to hear that my great expectations came from a prisoner I had helped in the past. When I introduced him to our guest, Herbert could not hide his dislike.

After my guest left, he said to me, "You look so pale and unwell, Handel. This must be a painful time for you."

"Herbert, I have to do something! He wants to spend even more money on me! What do I do?"

"You mean you won't accept any of his money from now on?"

"It's not possible! You know he's a criminal! What if his money is bad money? Where does it come from? And think about how much I owe him already! There's no way I can pay him back. Oh

---

① **in shape** 健康；健美。in bad shape 不健康

Herbert, I'm so glad to have you as a friend. I'm desperate①!" Herbert kindly pretended not to notice that I was almost crying.

"My dear Handel," he said, "you could always join my company, Clarrikers, if you want to pay him back what you owe him. I'm going to be a partner there soon, you know." Poor Herbert! He did not suspect that it was the prisoner's money that was helping him become a partner.

"But another thing," added Herbert. "Being a criminal this man must have a fierce and violent character. He's been looking forward to meeting you for over half his life. If you destroy his idea, his life will be worthless and he may get himself arrested."

"He would allow himself to be arrested and hanged," I agreed. "Yes, I've thought this was possible ever since he arrived. If that happened, I'd forever feel guilty②."

"You cannot destroy his dream. We must first get him out of England. Then you will explain to him that you can't, on your beliefs, accept his money

---

① **desperate** /'despərət/ *adj.* 绝望（拼命）的；不顾一切的
② **guilty** /'gɪltɪ/ *adj.* 有罪的；内疚的

anymore. I'll help you with everything. You can trust me." I gratefully shook Herbert's hand.

After breakfast the next morning we asked Magwitch to tell us about his past life.

"You promise to keep it secret, do you?" he said to us. "Well I'll make it short. In and out of prison—that's been my life. I don't remember my parents and I've no idea where I was born. I slept in fields, stole food, and sometimes I worked. I grew to be a man and it was about twenty years ago that I met Compeyson. If I ever meet him, I'd kill him now! He's the man I was fighting with the night the soldiers found me on the wetlands, Pip. He was a handsome and educated man that people wrongly took as① a gentleman. I was a partner in his business, and a dirty business it was, too. We would persuade rich people to invest money, and we used stolen banknotes and wrote false statements of money. Compeyson was a clever man, but what a wicked, cold heart he had! He was never blamed and would always get the profits."

"His former partner, Arthur, was living in

---

① **take (sth.) as...** （以某种方式）理解或解释……

Compeyson's house, but he was very ill. In fact he was dying. Some years ago, he and Compeyson had got a lot of money out of a rich lady, and Arthur kept dreaming about this lady. Late one night he came to the sitting-room door, pale and shaking like he'd just seen a ghost. "Compeyson," he cried. "She's there! In my room! All dressed in white and ready for our wedding! She says she wants revenge! You broke her heart, you did! And now she says I'm going to die for your wicked plans!"

"Compeyson and his wife put Arthur back to bed but at five o'clock in the morning we heard screams from his room. He died soon after that."

"I knew it was a mistake getting involved with Compeyson. We were both arrested for several crimes in the end. At the trial he lied and lied and I, being the criminal who was always in and out of prison, got fourteen years on the prison-ship. He, being the gentleman with important friends, only got seven years."

Magwitch had to breathe deeply to calm himself down. "I said to myself I'd smash his handsome face aboard the prison-ship. I was just about to when a guard came by. I escaped by diving into the river. That's how I ended up on the wetlands and in the churchyard. And then Pip, my boy, when you brought me food you told me Compeyson was on the wetlands too. So I hunted him down① and smashed his face. I was just going to take him back to the prison-ship when the soldiers caught us. Again his cleverness helped him. His punishment for escaping the ship was light. But because of my past life, I was sent to Australia for life."

"Is Compeyson dead?" I asked.

"I haven't heard any more of him," he said, shaking his head. "If he's alive though, then he hopes I'm dead, that's for certain②!"

Herbert passed me a note he had been writing. It said:

Arthur was the name of Miss Havisham's half-brother. Compeyson is the man who pretended to be in love with her and broke her heart.

---

① **hunt sb./sth. down** 对……追查到底。hunt down a criminal 追捕罪犯

② **for certain** 无疑地，确定地

Chapter 14
Pip Visits Estella and Miss Havisham Again

I felt I had to see both Estella and Miss Havisham before taking Magwitch abroad. When I arrived at Estella's London home, I found that she had gone to stay with Miss Havisham, and so I went by coach to the old town I knew so well.

I stopped at the hotel for breakfast on the way. I was not happy to discover Bentley Drummle there, and I could imagine his reason for visiting. When he noticed me, he immediately called out to the waiter, loud enough so I could hear, "Listen, you! The lady isn't going riding today. And remember, I'm not having dinner here tonight, I'll be at the lady's." Then Drummle smiled wickedly at me, knowing that his words cut me to the heart. He left, shouting for his horse.

I was so angry with him that if he had spoken Estella's name, I would have hit him. I was also depressed^① about my future and I could not eat my

---

① **depressed** /dɪˈprest/ *adj.* 降低的；沮丧的；抑郁的。depressing *adj.* 令人忧愁（沮丧）的

breakfast. I went straight to the old house instead.

There I found Miss Havisham and Estella sitting in the same room, with the candles burning the same as usual.

"Miss Havisham," I said, "I'm here to tell you that I'm as unhappy as you ever wanted me to be. I know now who has been paying for my education. I also know I shall never be rich, or important. Why this is so isn't my secret, but another person's." I stopped, wondering what to say next.

"Go on," said Miss Havisham. She looked very interested in my unhappiness.

"I thought it was you, Miss Havisham, who had given me my fortune! And you encouraged me in my mistake!"

"I've no reason to be kind to anybody after all I've suffered!" cried Miss Havisham angrily.

"Yes, you're right," I said quickly, to calm her. "But you've also encouraged your relations to believe that I am receiving some of your fortune after your death."

"And why shouldn't I?" she cried wildly.

"But Matthew Pocket and his son are different than the others. They aren't selfish or greedy, but generous and honest. I want you to know that."

She looked carefully at me. "And what is it you want for them?"

My cheeks were red when I replied. "I would like you to help Herbert become a partner in his company. Two years ago, I started paying for this myself—and I want to keep it a secret from him. But now I won't be able to continue the payments. I can't explain why. It's part of the other person's secret."

Miss Havisham looked first at the fire, and then at me again.

"What else do you have to say?" she asked.

I tried to control my trembling voice as I turned to Estella. "You know I love you, Estella," I said. "I have loved you dearly for a long time." She shook her head at me.

"I know I have no hope of ever being married to you, Estella. But let me say that I have loved you ever since I first saw you in this house. I think it cruel that Miss Havisham encouraged me to hope all this time while I was learning to be a gentleman, but I don't think she meant to be① unkind."

---

① **mean to do** 意欲，打算。mean doing 意味着；意思是

Estella was very calm. She replied, "What you said doesn't touch my heart. I've warned you that I can't feel love as you do, haven't I?"

"Yes," I answered miserably, "but I still don't believe it."

"It's how I was raised."

"Estella, I know that Bentley Drummle is in town here. Is he having dinner with you tonight?"

"Yes, it's true," she answered, a little surprised that I knew.

"But you don't love him, Estella!" I cried.

"Don't you listen to what I've said to you? I can never love anyone!" And then she added, "If you must know the truth, I'm going to marry him."

This was more than I could bear and I covered my face with my hands. After a moment I lifted my head and cried to her, "Don't give yourself away[①] to an animal like him! There must be others who love you who are a thousand times better. Any of them—but not Drummle!"

"I won't marry a man who wants me to love him. Drummle will do well enough as my husband.

---

① **give away**（有意或无意地）泄露某物或出卖某人

Anyway, you will soon forget me."

"Never, Estella! You are in every line I read, in every view I see, in every dream I dream. You are a part of me and until the last hour of my life, you will remain part of me. God bless you and God forgive you!" I kissed her hand and held it to my lips for a moment. Estella's beautiful face had a look of wonder as I was leaving, but Miss Havisham was staring at^① me with both pity and guilt.

I had to calm my feelings so I walked all the way back to London. The gates to my house at Temple were always closed, and I had to get the night watchman to let me inside. He gave me an envelope that was addressed to me. Inside, in Wemmick's handwriting, it said: "DON'T GO HOME."

---

① **stare at**（表示吃惊、茫然、傻愣愣地等）盯着看

Chapter 15
A Safe Place for Magwitch

I spent the night at a hotel, but I wasn't able to rest①. I kept worrying about the reasons for Wemmick's warning. Early the next morning I went to see him at the Castle. He said he had heard I was being watched at my house and that someone was looking for Magwitch. He also told me that Compeyson, Magwitch's enemy was alive and living in London. During my time away, Wemmick had told Herbert to move Magwitch to a safer place. Herbert had arranged to rent rooms for Magwitch in Clara's house near the open sea. She lived there with her father and there were many empty rooms. The house was further away from the middle of London than our home, and its location meant that we could easily take Magwitch abroad by boat from there.

"Magwitch is there now," said Wemmick, "and you can go to visit him tonight. But it's not safe to go back there after that. Remember, Mr. Pip," he

---

① **rest** /rest/ *vi.* 本意为"休息"，此处指"睡眠"。

added firmly, "remember to ask him for his cash. Don't let anything happen to his cash. You don't know what will happen to him and your future is uncertain, too."

I was not able to tell Wemmick how I felt about Magwitch's money, so I quietly agreed.

That evening I went to the house, and met Clara, Herbert's girlfriend. She was a very lovely girl, and she was obviously in love with Herbert. I thought of how lucky she and Herbert were, and I felt sad again when I thought of Estella.

Magwitch was much quieter than the last time I had seen him. He was grateful for all our arrangements. Also, he had become more gentle and likeable①. I was almost sorry to say goodbye to him later that night.

Life went on as normal for the next few weeks. Herbert went to work and visited Clara in the evenings. I had decided to keep a rowboat② near our house so that Herbert and I could visit Magwitch. I often rowed on the river, and waited for news from Wemmick.

① **likeable** /ˈlaɪkəbl/ *adj.* 可爱的；讨人喜欢的
② **rowboat** /ˈrəʊbəʊt/ *n.* 划艇（通常指非比赛用艇），英式英语为 rowing boat。

One evening I decided to go to the theatre. I knew that Mr. Wopsle was acting in a certain play, and I hoped that some entertainment would take my mind off of recent events. Mr. Wopsle noticed me in the audience, and he kept looking at me in a very strange way that I did not understand. After the play we met outside the theatre, and he immediately asked, "You didn't see that man sitting right behind you, Mr. Pip?"

I felt suddenly cold. "No. Who was he?" I asked.

"Remember that Christmas Day, Mr. Pip, when you were a young boy? We had the soldiers come to the house and then we went on to the wetlands with them to find a couple of escaped prisoners. Well, one of them was sitting behind you, looking over your shoulder during the play tonight."

"Do you know which one it was?" I asked, holding my breath.

"The one whose face was bleeding when we arrived," he answered.

Compeyson was still following me! I knew then Magwitch was in greater danger① than we

---

① **danger** /ˈdeɪndʒə/ *n.* 危险 1) danger of sth. 有某种危险；2) danger to sb./sth. 对……有危险（危害）；3) be in danger 处在危险中

imagined. Later that evening I discussed the problem with Herbert, and we promised each other to be more careful.

A week later I met Mr. Jaggers in the street. As we hadn't seen each other in a while, he invited me to dinner at his house that evening. When I arrived, Wemmick was also there. Mr. Jaggers told me Miss Havisham had asked to see me on business, so I agreed to go there the next day.

Then Jaggers said, "Well, Pip! Our friend Drummle has won himself a great prize! He has just married Estella!"

Even though I had been expecting this news for a while, it still came as a terrible shock.

"I'd like to see," continued Jaggers, "who will be the stronger one in the marriage—the wife or the husband? He may have to beat her—"

"Surely he wouldn't do something like that!" I cried.

"Perhaps, but perhaps not. She is certainly more intelligent than him, so we shall see."

Right after Jaggers said this, I noticed the housekeeper putting a dish on the table. I looked hard at her. I knew those eyes and those hands. I had seen them somewhere, along with the same expression very recently! Suddenly I was absolutely certain that this woman was Estella's mother.

Later, after Wemmick and I had left Jaggers' house together, I asked him about Jaggers' housekeeper. He told me that, many years ago, his housekeeper had become jealous of her husband and another woman. Later, the other woman was murdered and Jaggers' housekeeper was accused of murdering her. Jaggers was her lawyer at the trial, and he managed to convince everyone that she was not strong enough to have killed the woman. She was also believed to have killed her three-year-old daughter, who had strangely disappeared. But because of Jaggers' clever arguing and skill, she was judged innocent[①] of murder. She left her husband after the trial and became Jaggers' housekeeper.

---

① **innocent** /ˈɪnəsənt/ *adj.* 无辜的；清白的；无害的

Chapter 16
Miss Havisham Realizes Pip's Suffering

M iss Havisham's house looked darker than ever when I arrived the next day. Suddenly, I realized how lonely she was now that Estella had gone. She looked sadly at me.

"Tell me, Pip," she said, stretching out her hand to me, "how may I help your friend? You mentioned something about it the last time you were here."

I explained my agreement with Clarrikers and how Herbert was to be[①] made a partner. Nine hundred pounds still had to be paid to the company before they would do so.

"Will you be happier if I pay this?"

"Much happier."

"And how about yourself, Pip? Can't I do anything for you?"

"No. There is nothing you can do for me," I

---

① **be to do** 的含义有多种，包括责任、义务、可能性等，此处表示"安排，意向或目的"。

answered.

She handed me a written cheque. "Mr. Jaggers will give you the money you need. And—here, Pip," she said, handing me another piece of paper, "here is a note with only my name on. I hope one day you can write under it 'I forgive her.' "

"Oh Miss Havisham," I said, "I can do it now. I can't be bitter with anyone because I know we all make mistakes."

"What have I done, Pip!" she suddenly cried, dropping to her knees in front of me. "It was wrong to raise her so! I should never have brought up Estella like that, or allowed you to be hurt!"

"What is done is done, but please tell me something about Estella. How and why did you adopt her?"

"I never knew who her parents were," she said quietly. "I wanted a child of my own, and so I asked Jaggers to find a little girl for me to adopt. He brought Estella here. She was only about three when she arrived at my house."

As we had nothing more to say to one another, I left. But walking through the old garden I had a strange feeling that something was wrong. I decided to run back upstairs to check on① Miss Havisham. When I opened the door of her room, I saw her sitting close to the fire. Suddenly, the room was lit by a great flame. She came rushing towards me, screaming, with her hair and clothes on fire. I quickly covered her with my coat and somehow managed to put out② the flames with my hands.

I called for a doctor, and he cleaned her burns as best he could. They placed her bed on the great dining table, where her wedding cake had once been. She lay there, half-conscious and covered with a white sheet. I could not stay because I had to return to London, so I left her in the care of the doctor and several nurses.

My hands and right arm had been badly burnt by the fire. Though I was in great pain, I needed to know if Magwitch was safe, and so I went straight to find Herbert.

As he gently put bandages③ on my hands, Herbert assured me that everything was fine. "He

---

① **check on** 检查（确保安全、正确、满意或处于良好状态）

② **put out** 扑灭；使……停止燃烧

③ **bandage** /ˈbændɪdʒ/ *n.* 绷带

seems much more pleasant than before," he said. "I actually quite like him now. Yesterday he was telling me about his interesting past. Do you know, he was once married to a young woman who was jealous of another woman. There was a fight, and his wife killed the woman. But his wife was never punished for the murder because she had a very clever lawyer who convinced everyone she was innocent. She and Magwitch had a daughter, and Magwitch loved his daughter dearly. But both his wife and his child disappeared after the trial. He thought that his wife must have killed their daughter."

Trying to control my excitement, I asked Herbert how old the daughter was.

"If she had lived, she would be about your age."

"Herbert," I said, "do I look ill or mad or anything[①]?"

"No," replied Herbert, "but you do look a little excited."

"Listen to what I know, Herbert. Magwitch is Estella's father!"

The next day I felt ill and weak because of my burns. I went straight to Jaggers' office. He

---

① **or something (anything)** 口语，意为 "或诸如此类的事物"

admitted to me that his housekeeper's daughter was Estella, adopted by Miss Havisham to give her the chance of a better life. But he did not know that Magwitch was Estella's father.

Chapter 17
Pip Is Close to Death

M r. Jaggers paid me the money from Miss Havisham's check and I took the nine hundred pounds to Clarrikers, feeling happy that Herbert's future, at least, was safe. Clarrikers had decided to send Herbert to India, so that they could open a new office there. I felt rather sad that while helping my old friend, I would also be losing him.

Wemmick told us it would be best to move Magwitch out of the country during the middle of the week. We decided to row our boat down to Clara's house on Wednesday to collect① Magwitch. From there we could continue rowing down the river to Essex, where we could place Magwitch on board one of the foreign ships sailing from London to Germany or Holland. We hoped for luck so that no one would notice us. Because my hands were still too painful from the burns, Startop agreed to row

---

① **collect** /kəˈlekt/ *vt.* 此处指领（带）走（某人）

for me.

However, when I went back to our rooms that Monday, I found a letter that was addressed to me with no return address. It had been delivered by hand. It said:

I have information about your guest. If you want it, you should come tonight or tomorrow night to the old house that is near the lime[①] *factory on the wetlands. You must come alone. Tell no one.*

I did not have time to think about what to do. I rushed out again and barely[②] made the afternoon coach.

I stopped in town only to ask about Miss Havisham's health. News was that she was still very ill. Then I walked quickly on to the dark lonely wetlands. I soon arrived at the lime factory. The workmen had all gone home and there was no one in the factory. I pushed open the door of the old house, thinking that it was empty. To my surprise I found a bed, a table and a candle inside. Suddenly

---

① **lime** /laɪm/ *n.* (熟) 石灰
② **barely** /'beəlɪ/ *adv.* 刚好；不超过；仅仅；几乎不

my candle was blown out①. I was attacked from behind and before I could fight back my arms were tied close to my sides with a thick rope. The pain in my burned arm was terrible. After a moment the candle was lit again, and I saw my attacker—Orlick! I could tell he had been drinking, and I knew I was in a very dangerous situation.

"Now," he said fiercely, "I've got you!"

"Why did you bring me here? What do you want from me?" I asked.

"Don't you know?" he replied, drinking straight from a bottle. "You're my enemy. I lost that job at Miss Havisham's because of what you said. Biddy would have liked me but she liked you better. All my life you've been in my way②. Even Joe loved you more. And now I'm going to take your life! Tonight you're going to die!"

I knew Orlick was serious and I felt I was looking down into my own grave. There were no possible ways of escape.

"I don't want anything left of you after I'm done," he said. "I'll put your body in the fire oven.

① **blow out** 吹灭（熄），被吹熄
② **in one's way** 阻碍或造成不便

In the morning there'll be nothing left, not your clothes, not even your body."

I realized that in my hurry I had not told anybody where I was going. Nobody would even know where to begin looking for me.

"Another thing," he continued, smiling cruelly, "I hit your sister with the iron chain that prisoner left on the wetlands, but I did it because I hated you! It's your fault your sister died the way she did!" He drank again. I watched the level of the liquid go down and down. I felt that when he finished the bottle, my life would end.

"I know all about that prisoner you're hiding. I've been waiting and watching everything you do outside your rooms and on the stairs. You even fell over me① once. My friend's going to tell the police all about him. Yes, Compeyson will make sure he's hanged when you're dead!"

The last of the bottle's rum went down his throat, and picking up his hammer, he rushed towards me. I shouted as loudly as I could, determined to fight. Suddenly the door was knocked

---

① **fall over sb./sth.** 在行走时脚碰到某人（某物）而跌倒或打趔趄。而 fall over oneself 表示 "动作笨拙"。

down and Herbert and Startop rushed in. Orlick, with a violent shout, quickly jumped over the table, through an open window and escaped into the night.

In my hurry, I had dropped Orlick's letter in my room in London. When my friends found it, they suspected something wicked, so they came straight to find me on the wetlands. They luckily arrived just in time.

They took me back to London later that night. Because of our situation with Magwitch, we decided to not tell the police. My friends looked after me carefully all the next day, so that, even though my burnt arm was still hurting and I was still very weak, I would be strong enough for the planned journey on Wednesday.

Chapter 18
Magwitch's Story Ends

W e set out cheerfully down the river on a cold bright morning. I steered[①] the boat while Herbert and Startop rowed. Magwitch was waiting for us at Clara's house. He was wrapped in a big, dark coat.

"My dear boy!" he said, laying his hand on my shoulder as he sat down heavily in the boat. "Thank you!"

We rowed eastward all day, keeping a look round to make sure that no one was following us. Magwitch was smoking his pipe and watching the water. He seemed quite happy.

At one point[②] he said, "You don't know what a pleasure it is, Pip, to be with you, my dear boy, in the open air."

"By tomorrow you'll be completely safe and free," I said.

"I hope so, dear boy. But it's hard to look into

① **steer** /stɪə/ *vt.* 操纵（船、汽车等）行驶方向；驾驶
② **at one point** 突然。point 指（特定）时刻，瞬间

the future, isn't it? It's like looking for the bottom of a muddy river. It just can't be done." He was silent after that.

The sky was getting dark and we decided to spend the night at a little pub by the riverside. There were no other guests so it seemed safe, but during our conversation with the owner of the pub, he asked us some questions which made us worry.

"Did you see that boat go past here, gentlemen? It was rowed by four men, with two others on board. It's been going up and down this river several times today. It could be a Customs boat."

We discussed this information in whispers after he left us alone. We finally decided to go to bed and then set out early the next morning to catch the ship to Hamburg. I woke[①] early, and looked out of the window to see the weather. I saw two men looking at our boat, but I didn't wake Herbert or Startop. I thought they needed their rest after rowing all day yesterday.

In the late morning we rowed our boat to the center of the river. We could see the ship to Hamburg

---

① **wake** /weɪk/ *vi.* 醒来；唤醒；使觉醒

approaching. Magwitch and I said goodbye to Herbert and Startop and then picked up our bags. We were ready to stop the ship and get on board. Suddenly from nowhere a boat rowed by four men appeared and came out very fast toward us. A fifth man was steering, and a sixth man, whose face we could not see because it was hidden in his coat, whispered instructions to the man who was steering. They all looked hard at us.

"Stop! We know you have a prisoner who's just returned from Australia," shouted the man who was steering. "His name is Abel Magwitch. I'm a Customs officer[①] and I'm here to arrest him!"

Their boat quickly arrived to ours. Meanwhile, the ship for Hamburg was coming closer and soon would be on top of us. The ship's captain shouted to stop engines, but his order was too late. At the same moment, the Customs officer laid his hand on Magwitch's shoulder, and Magwitch pulled the coat off the other man in the boat. It was Compeyson! I watched as he fell backwards into the water, with his face full of fear. Then the huge Hamburg ship

① **a Customs officer** customs 为复数形式，表"海关，关税"，而专司收税的政府部门"海关"的表达为 the Customs，单数 custom 则为"风俗，习俗，个人习惯"。

hit our tiny boat with a great crash. The Customs officers somehow managed to get me, with Herbert and Startop, on board their boat, but our boat sank, and the two prisoners had disappeared.

We soon discovered Magwitch in the water. He was badly injured, and we gently pulled him into the boat. He told me that he had fallen into the water together with Compeyson, and then the ship crashed① into him. I believed what he said. There was no sign of Compeyson, but his dead body was found up the river several days later.

Magwitch had to wait in prison for his trial. I had with high hopes arranged for Jaggers to be his lawyer. But Jaggers warned me that Magwitch would probably die as there was almost no hope of proving him innocent. As for Magwitch's thick wallet, it was handed over to the police, which annoyed Wemmick to no end.

"Really, Mr. Pip, you lost so much cash!" he said, "You see, Compeyson was determined to get his revenge. He knew that once the police found out you couldn't have saved Magwitch. But the

___
① **crash** /kræʃ/ *vi.* 突然倒下；撞击发出声响；使猛撞。crash into sth. 撞到某物

cash could certainly have been saved. That's the difference. But I must ask you something, Mr. Pip. Would you join me for a walk on Monday morning?"

I thought it's a very strange request. Though I did not really feel like accepting[①], especially after all I had been through, he politely insisted.

Early Monday morning I arrived at the Castle. After a glass of rum and milk, we set out on our walk.

"Well, look here!" said Wemmick suddenly, "Here's a church! Why don't we go in?" And when we entered, there was another surprise.

"Well, well!" he said again. "Look what I've just found in my pockets!" He had "found" two pairs of white gloves. "Let's put these on, shall we?" His post-box mouth was open as wide as it could possibly be, and I began to suspect something. And when I saw the Aged come in with a lady, I knew I was right.

"Well, well!" said Wemmick, still pretending to be surprised, "here's the Aged, and Miss Skiffins! Let's have a wedding!"

---

① **feel like doing sth.** 想要做某事

And so Wemmick married Miss Skiffins, and we celebrated the marriage afterwards at a little pub near the church.

I was happy for Wemmick and delighted that he carried out① his wedding in such an interesting manner, but I could not stop worrying about Magwitch. He was moved to the prison hospital because of his bad injuries. I visited him there every day. I read to him, and talked to him, and did everything to make him comfortable. But day by day I could see he was becoming weaker, although he never complained about his health. In the eyes of the prison guards he was a dangerous criminal, but to me he was a poor and unfortunate man, who still had some goodness② in him. I could not leave him now.

What Jaggers had said was proved right at the trial. The judge ordered that Magwitch must be hanged as he was a prisoner sent away for life who had returned. I did not want to accept this terrible punishment, so I wrote to all the important people I could think of, asking for help and mercy for Mag-

---

① **carry out** 实施，执行；完成；进行
② **goodness** /ˈɡʊdnɪs/ n. (不可数名词) 善良；美德；(对某人) 好意

witch. But I was refused. There was no way to fight the law.

Magwitch was getting much worse by the day. Sometimes he could not speak when I visited him and he would just press my hand. I usually found him lying on his bed, looking calmly up at the white ceiling. One evening as I entered his room, he smiled weakly at me.

"Dear boy," he said, "you're never late."

"I don't have any moments of time to lose. I'm only allowed to visit you for a certain time," I said.

"Thank you, dear boy. God bless you! You've never left me, dear boy!" He had spoken his last words.

I placed my hand on his chest and remembered that I had wanted to leave him once before. He put both his hands on mine.

"Dear Magwitch, you must listen to me. You had a child once, a young daughter, who you loved and lost." He pressed my hand gently in agreement①. "She's alive. She's a lady and very beautiful. And I love her!"

①　**agreement** /əˈɡriːmənt/ *n.* 协定（议）；一致

He was too weak to speak, but he managed to lift my hand to his lips. Then his eyes looked peacefully up at the white ceiling again. Slowly they closed and his head dropped quietly on to his chest.

Chapter 19
A Wedding

All these events① made me seriously ill for several weeks. Because Herbert was abroad, on business for Clarrikers, there was nobody to look after me. But Joe had heard about my illness and come to London to take care of me.

After I was a little better, he told me about the local news. Miss Havisham had died, leaving all of her fortune to Estella, except for 4,000 pounds, which she gave to Matthew Pocket. Orlick had been arrested for stealing money, which he stole from Pumblechook's house. I was glad to see that dear old Joe seemed just the same, but as I got better, he began to think it proper to start calling me "sir" again. Then I got up one morning and saw that he had gone.

I decided to return to the village to thank him for all his help. Also, I wanted to carry out a plan I had been thinking about for a long time. I wanted

---

① **event** /ɪ'vent/ *n.* 事件［辨］1) event 多指重大事件，尤指历史事件；2) incident 多指较小事件，特指事变，争端；3) occurrence 多指偶然发生的事，尤指普通的事。

to ask Biddy to marry me, and I believed I would be happy with her. I went by coach to the old town, just as I had so many times before, and walked to the iron workshop. But as I came closer, I didn't hear the sound of Joe's hammer. I also noticed fresh white curtains at the windows and bright flowers everywhere. Suddenly I saw Biddy and Joe standing at the door, arm in arm.

"Pip!" cried Biddy happily, running up to kiss me. "Pip, it's my wedding day, and I'm married to Joe!"

The shock was too much for me. They helped me into the house and let me rest in a chair. They were both so happy that I had, by accident, come to make their day perfect and complete. I was very glad that I had never spoken earlier of my plan to Joe when he was looking after me.

"Dear Biddy," I said, "you have married the best husband in the whole world."

"It's not possible to love him more than I do," she replied.

"And dear Joe, you have married the best wife in the world! She will make you as happy as even you deserve to be, dear good Joe!" Joe put his arm

over his eyes. "And Joe and Biddy," I continued, "I want to thank you for all you've done for me. From the bottom of my heart I thank you. Tell me you forgive① me for being ungrateful, and not being good. And try to think better of me in the future!"

"Oh dear old Pip," said Joe, "God knows we forgive you, if there is anything to forgive!"

I left the iron workshop, returned to London, and started a new life working as a clerk for Clarrikers, Herbert's company. Soon I was sent to take charge of② the new office in India, while Herbert returned to England to marry his Clara.

Herbert and his wife invited me to live with them in India, and we stayed there for many years. In the end I also became a partner in the company. We worked hard and honestly, and made good profits.

Although I wrote to them regularly, it was not until eleven years later that I returned to England to see Biddy and Joe again. One evening in December I gently pushed open the old kitchen

---

① **forgive** /fə'gɪv/ *vt.* 原谅，饶恕

② **take charge of (sth.)** 控制（掌管）……；承担责任。in charge (of sb./sth.) 控制（支配）……；负责

door to the house, and there, sitting by the fire next to Joe, in my old place, was—Pip! Joe and Biddy had given their son my name and he even looked a lot like me. They had also had a little daughter, and were the happiest of parents.

"Dear Pip," asked Biddy one night quietly after supper, "have you quite forgotten her? Tell me, as an old friend."

"My dear Biddy, I will never forget her. But that was all a dream from long ago that has passed!"

I was secretly planning to go alone and revisit Miss Havisham's old house. As for Estella[①], I had heard that her husband had been very cruel to her. They had separated, and later he had died. This was two years ago. Perhaps she had remarried by now.

The old house was no longer there. It had been knocked down, and there was nothing left but piles of stones in the garden. I walked sadly around in the moonlight, until suddenly I saw a woman in the shadows. I went closer and then—

"Estella!" I cried.

"You recognize me? But I have changed a lot,"

---

① **as for sb./sth.** 至于某人或某物

she answered.

She was older, but still very beautiful. She had changed, too—I had never before seen soft light in those once proud eyes, or felt a friendly touch from her once cold hand.

"How strange, Estella! After so many years, we meet by chance exactly where we first met!"

"Yes, it's strange. Although the land belongs to me, I haven't been here for years. But tell me, you still live abroad?"

"Yes, I still do. I have a good business in India."

"I've often thought of you. Since—my husband— died, I have given you a place in my heart."

"You have always had a place in my heart," I answered.

There was silence for a few moments.

"I didn't think I would be saying goodbye to you here," she said.

"It's painful saying goodbye, Estella."

"Last time you said, 'God bless you, God forgive you!' You could say that to me now, now that I understand how much you loved me. I have suffered, and now I am a better person. Please tell me we are friends." She spoke more eagerly① and sincerely than I had ever heard her speak before.

"We are friends," I said, and took her hand in mine.

"We will continue to be friends, even when we are apart," said Estella.

We walked, hand in hand, leaving the old garden behind. Just as the morning mist was rising when I first left the iron workshop long ago, so the evening mist was rising now. In the clear moonlight, I saw no shadow of another separation from her.

---

① **eagerly** /ˈiːɡəlɪ/ *adv.* 热切地〔辨〕1) eager 指有进取的热情，"热切（急切、渴望）的"；2) ardent 有"炽热的"含义；3) enthusiastic 有兴趣而激发热情的